C000147420

First published 1995

ISBN 0 9515738 7 X

Published by Footmark Publications,
12 The Bourne,
Fleet,
Hampshire GU13 9TL

Typesetting by Distinguished Data Ltd,
Floods Farm Cottage,
Dogmersfield,
Hampshire RG27 8TD
Tel: 01252 850311

Printed by Rodek Printing,
Unit 5 Grove Park,
Mill Lane,
Alton,
Hampshire GU34 2QG
Tel: 01420 86386

*The front cover is based on a painting of Home Farm, Cove, by the well-known
local artist Terry Harrison.*

Contents

Maps

(Facing) Frontispiece illustration: Aerial view of Cove in 1945

Arthur Lunn was born in Cove and except for wartime service in the Royal Engineers has spent most of his life in the village. His recollections of earlier this century capture the atmosphere of Cove admirably and he gives a real feel for the characters and events involved. His shrewd observations add colour to the account.

In those days many locals, despite the undoubted harder conditions endured, mostly seemed to have the time to spare to know each other. Sadly nowadays the faster pace of life largely prevents this.

I also grew up in Cove, but only got to know Arthur well recently because of our shared interest in local history. However this book is not a dry list of facts, but gives readers a good idea of what life was like. It will be enjoyed by both older residents and those who now live in the much busier Cove.

The author, as a keen amateur historian, poses two questions: Why is the village of Cove so named? What is the origin of Tower Hill? He quite rightly regards this as the most important part of his book. His original research has uncovered some remarkable facts concerning the origins of Cove that have so far eluded others. His speculations based on these discoveries are thought provoking and readers must decide for themselves on their validity. Was Cove and Tower Hill with its scattered sarsen stones once an important prehistoric centre possibly ranking with Stonehenge?

Bob Rose   *Fleet 1995*

Preface

Why 'Our Hampshire Cove' when the title might well have been 'The one and only Cove'? It so happens that somewhere in the depth of Devon there is another even smaller village bearing the same name.

What is most surprising is that there are not many more 'Coves'. For several columns in the Oxford Dictionary are devoted to explaining the different usage of this word. One meaning of the word 'cove' is 'a recess among hills or woods'. Surely this would apply to thousands of rural sites all over the English countryside.

This then is the story of 'our' Cove, a village tucked away in the top right-hand corner of the County of Hampshire.

Arthur Lunn
Tower Hill,
Cove, Hampshire
March 1995

Introduction

Cove – the very name is old from way back before the Domesday Book and the great English King Alfred. Its name unchanged by Roman invaders or Saxon settlers. Simple without the added and altered 'bergas', 'leys' and 'hams'. A name with just a hint of prehistoric pagan roots. For a 'Cove' was one of those Stone Age places of assembly, worship and sacrifice.

For years historians and archaeologists have failed to make good use of the opportunities they have had to delve into the ancient history of Cove. Little has been written apart from a pamphlet entitled 'Cove Old and New 880-1925' by the then Vicar's wife, Mrs May Watson and Mrs Callingham. So it is left to a 'dreamer' with an imagination not shackled by science or an excess of learning to 'have a go'.

The writer started what is best described as a country village education at Tower Hill School when it was only a wooden hut and 'finished' under the Gilderdales, Rolls and Reynolds at the 'big' Cove School. He learnt respect for others and for nature in the 1st Cove Troop of Boy Scouts and comes from a poor but respectable local family that goes back to the early 1800s. Great-great-grandfather George Lunn married Mary Barr on the 26 November 1818. Mary Lunn died in 1864 aged 66; she lived in and was buried from Farnborough Workhouse, Workhouse Lane, now Union Street – you can't get much poorer or more local than that.

Respectability is claimed by the knowledge that through 150 years of family history, there has only been a single hint of illegitimacy, Rose Elizabeth in 1872. This as any old Cove resident will tell you, is well above the average respectability for the village.

This present member of the family left school at the age of 14 on a Wednesday, started work the following day a Thursday and for fifty years absorbed local ways and customs. It was this unique opportunity of meeting people whilst working in their homes that prompted this collection of stories.

The main object of this book is to delve into the realms of imagination and speculate on what might or could have been many years ago. But for the sake of younger readers, the writer has been persuaded to begin with Cove as it was a mere 60 to 80 years back into the past and then to go on exploring the village as it might have been in 2000 BC.

All through these stories you will find reference to the prehistoric sarsen stones, for these form a continuous, solid and indestructible link through the ages. As they are still to be found about Tower Hill, they provide visible evidence to what could have been our pagan past.

Let us look first at the geography and lay-out of Cove village. Think not of it in its present urban sprawl, but as a close-knit community of less than one hundred families. In those days it consisted of 200 acres of farm-land and 2000 acres of open common. It was almost completely surrounded by water and marsh-land; the only access was along a sandy ridge a little over 200 yards across, the width of today's Victoria Road Cemetery.

We do not have to go back thousands of years to know how deep and sluggish were the streams draining the Blackwater Valley. For well within living memory, the water-table over most of the land surrounding Cove was only a few inches below ground. Many will remember how every winter floods stretched across the fields from Prospect Road to Fernhill Road and how those who first moved into the newly-built houses on West Heath were surprised to find that in their gardens the water was only six inches below the surface. Now with clearance and deepening by Thames Conservancy, the water level in Cove Brook has gone down and down. Unfortunately some house foundations have followed.

The whole area to the south of Victoria Road from behind the Tumble Down Dick and at the back of Spooner's Forge as far along as the small bridge in Arrow Road, was impassable marsh-land. Cove men employed in the 'Factory' before 1914 either crossed this bridge or took the long route up to the Clockhouse.

It was only when Rafborough was built that 'short cuts' along the 'Black Paths' were made on raised causeways of ash and cinders from the Factory furnaces. One path is still used, now smooth tarmac for pedestrian and bicycle traffic. It goes from Marrowbrook Lane to Invincible Road, where the old path crossed the lines carrying the railway from Farnborough Station siding right into the centre of the RAE as the 'Factory' became.

The path continued and still follows the same route where it skirted the Tank Corps sports ground and finished up at Pinehurst Gate, the RAE's 'back door'. The hops that once grew in profusion all over the fields crossed by this path, still persist in bearing their yearly harvest. Unused and unpicked for almost a century and lacking hop poles, they now cling to trees and telephone posts. Gone too are the deep ditches beside the path, they, like the old Marrow Brook, now flow through pipes many feet below the ground.

Chapter One
A Guide to the Long-Lost History of Cove

T o appreciate fully the mystery and history of Cove, the reader must first know of the sarsen stones and how they appear under varying names in many different places.

Through the ages these ancient stones have been called Grey Wethers, Sarsdon or Sarston, Druid Stones or Saracen Stones. This last name suggests strange foreigners. But modern archaeologists favour the title Sarsen, from the Saxon *Sar-stan* or troublesome stone, for this is how the earliest tillers of the soil found them.

In the 1970s, the Society of Antiquaries undertook a careful and detailed survey of such stones in Hampshire. Some 700, on 303 different sites were found and listed either as single standing stones or in groups. Unfortunately Cove's contribution to the past was overlooked; a pity for the 1,500 sarsen stones on or around Tower Hill would have added considerably to this total. This exclusion is understandable, for the Cove stones lacked the sheer size and grandeur of a Stonehenge or an Avebury circle. Our stones tend to be much smaller and more scattered, ranging from loaf-size to a quarter of a ton.

It might also be of interest to understand the 'when, how and where' in the life-story of sarsens; for many of these large stones still lie beneath the Chobham Ridge where they were first formed many million years ago. Unlike marble laid down when the Earth was fiery and molten, sarsen is a 'gentle' stone evolved through quiet natural stages when the world was warm, damp and still.

The plateau we now know as Chobham Ridges and the Fox Hills, was once a wide expanse of fine quartzose sand containing silicates, over-laid by a thick mat of organic vegetable sediment that provided acidic reaction in a damp still atmosphere. Results: a mixture of water, sand and silicates, almost the same ingredients as modern man-made concrete, in a vast slab up to a yard thick, smooth, except for a few prehistoric root marks proof in themselves of a quiet beginning.

In time the sarsen stone surface was buried beneath 12 feet of glacial gravel, it is still down there; now and then when men scratch the surface large blocks are uncovered. For anyone interested there is said to be a single slab 16 feet by 8 feet by 3 feet in the bottom of a gravel pit to the east of Blackdown Barracks.

Along the steep western face of this plateau, stones were 'washed down'. These were the source of local sarsen stone for prehistoric builders who had no tools to quarry. Stone Age man had many objects of worship and sacrifice and most revered was the Sun, giver of light and heat; so it was to the Sun that most 'temples' were raised. The earliest formation was of three large upright slabs like a 'sentry-box' with the open side facing the rising sun, this came to be called a 'Cove'.

Quoting from books that have been written about the veneration of stones, some as far back as the Old Testament:

'In the centre of Avebury stone circle are three megaliths in a special arrangement known as a COVE. The back stone faced the local mid-winter sunrise, which is close to 130 degrees'.

'The COVE is plainly a sacred construction'.

Even before standing stones were raised, large flat stones may have marked the ancient shrines. When ordered to 'cast down' the old stones, early Christians simply built their churches upon them. In early Christian times, the Venerable Bede records that Augustine of Canterbury was advised by Pope Gregory to use the sites of pagan shrines for Christian worship. By the end of the 13th century, Bishop John Pontoise of Winchester had published an edict banning the veneration of stones, logs, trees or wells.

Heavy sarsens from this Surrey ridge could have been placed upon log rafts, floated down the deep, sluggish Blackwater River and dragged to where the churches of Eversley, Yateley and Heckfield now stand. For in or under each of these churches are large, flat sarsen stones.

These then are some of the facts, fiction and imagination needed to make the whole idea of Cove's prehistory believable.

We can only guess at the past by examining the present, so let us look at what is left of the sarsen stones of Tower Hill which is close to the junction of Victoria Road and Marrowbrook Lane. This useful stone has been re-used and scattered, so it would be a fair assumption that little more than ten percent still remain on or near its original site.

Most are in the garden of a house in Victoria Road; many of these have been piled to form the front garden wall, others have been scattered about the garden, some 700 in all. In the grounds of a house in Tower Hill (close to St Christopher's Church), both above and below the surface, are another 500 sarsen stones, the larger ones weighing up to half a ton.

This then is the evidence that some mysterious ancient stones were accumulated on Tower Hill and may well have given their name to the village of Cove.

Chapter Two
Cove Farms

F ew signs remain of the many farms that once gave employment to the majority of men in the village. Not only the men, for women, boys and girls all found work in the dairies, hop fields and meadows, especially in late summer when the harvest came.

Elderly 'Covites' claim to be able to put names to some 15 or 16 different farms in or around the village, but I will concentrate on the few, some only faintly visible, that I recall from the 1920s and 1930s.

Let us start right in the middle of the village with **Home Farm**, said to date back to 1741. Later it became the Vicarage and now the old house has been converted to individual flats. The entrance to the farmyard was up what is now St Christopher's Road.

In the 1800s, Home Farm was worked by Farmer James Lunn when most fields were given over to grazing and hops. It was the centre of Cove village life, for not only was it the largest farm, but here they also grew and dried the hops that made up the local brew. Two circular brick hop drying kilns stood at the back of the farmyard near the pathway behind The Tradesmans Arms; this spot is now occupied by 6 & 7 St Christopher's Place.

There were prolonged arguments amongst the village 'elders' as to whether the old photograph shows Home Farm. The reasons for the identification are as follows. Firstly the typically local, twin-gabled 'M' shaped roof and end chimney stacks, although added to and altered during the past one hundred years, are still clearly visible. An 1870 map confirms the farm's squared yard surrounded by out-buildings and also the round duck pond in the middle. The three men with a horse and cart appear to be 'mucking out' the pond. The large tree on the right looks suspiciously like the old walnut tree that was felled in the 1930s to make space for the present-day St Christopher's Church. The most significant evidence is revealed by a close examination, this shows in the background on the left the conical roof of the oast-house used for drying hops. By coincidence another nearby building of similar shape and age – the Queens Head public house in Marrowbrook Lane – was ruled out for it has never opened on to a farmyard.

Southwood Farm was on the site of a much older building. On old maps it is sometimes called 'Southward'. It is now The Monkey Puzzle public house. Farmer 'Siddie' Groves built a long straight causeway from the farm to Hazel Avenue, crossing the so often flooded water-meadows.

(Top) Originally Home Farm, later Cove Vicarage, with its 'M' shaped roof, two gable ends and chimneys typical of many older Cove houses. The new wing built across the far end contained the servants' quarters. (Bottom) Home Farm, Cove – about 1880.

The Queens Head public house also shows the 'M' shaped roof and chimneyed gables. Both buildings could date back over two centuries and several equally old Cove houses have been demolished well within living memory.

This raised drive proved a great help to village children who walked up to the milking sheds to collect the family's jug of skimmed milk, cost 1d, half the price of a pint bought at the door from the milkman's churn. Each generation bemoans the rising cost of living; our parents in the 1920s thought a 1d a high price when they once paid 3d for a bucketful from the same farm.

Brookhouse Farm was halfway along Hazel Avenue near to a footpath coming across the fields from The Tradesmans Arms. This path carried on across two water-meadows, spanning Cove Brook on two stout planks with 'pinch' posts at each end to stop straying cattle. Finally the path crossed Siddie Grove's field to reach Ively Cottages. This part of the path got ploughed up each year and the first villager to walk over it re-established the right of way. By the early 1920s there was little left of Brookhouse Farm, but its name can still be seen on a nearby street sign. All that remained was a tumbled heap of old bricks, once the farmhouse fireplace, and an ancient pear tree still bearing small sweet fruit.

There were two other farms in Hazel Avenue. Of course in those days it was not important enough to be known as an avenue or to take its name from Mick Yeoman's Hazels Farm. It was simply known as the Farm Lane.

(Top) Southwood Farm, as it was in the times of Farmer 'Siddie' Groves, surrounded by flood water from over-flowing of Cove Brook. The two large barns, built out of line with each other, were an unmistakable feature. (Bottom) The same scene today: the flooded meadow is now a golf course, the big black barns have gone to make room for a car-park. The 'monkey puzzle' tree is taller with a bushy top and has given its name to the public house that was once Southwood or Southward Farm.

The 'ring road' round Cove was Marrowbrook Lane from New Road (later Victoria Road) and Hazel Avenue to where it joined Cove Road opposite Twitchens Post Office, now No 102 Cove Road.

Another farm in Hazel Avenue was **Eelmoor** where old Mrs Arrow and her son Eddie kept pigs. When demolished a few years ago to make way for new houses in Meadow Close, it was found to be built over the site of a mediaeval settlement. Those old-time builders knew all about local conditions when they put their rude huts on wooden piles and so high off the boggy ground. Arrow's pigs enjoyed a diet of acorns from the many oak trees that still line Cove lanes. Local children supplemented their weekly sugar intake by collecting bags of these acorns to exchange for 'twists' of sweets at Mr Cook's shop next to the farm. Prudent grocers did not waste bags on children's sweets when cones of newspaper would do just as well. The pigs were kept penned in, or should it be 'styed', within the farmyard, whereas years ago they would have had the run of the oak woods upon Cove Common living off acorns and beech mast. For it was the grubbing pigs and trampling cattle that kept the meadows clear of encroaching trees and shrubs. One only has to look at the small water-meadow beside Arrow Road to see how quickly grassland can revert back to woodland. So the pigs were kept within the yard and fed upon swill. Each day Eddie Arrow took his horse and cart round to the nearby Army barracks returning with two barrels slopping over with smelly pig swill. It was the firm belief of many an old soldier that the preparation of Army food was to ensure a steady income for the Sergeant Cook by maintaining this by-product. That was of course long before the formation of that splendid body of men, the Army Catering Corps.

Parsonage Farm was not strictly in the village, it being well out on the West Heath just off Trunk Lane. It was farmed by the Harvey family who mostly kept pigs. There was also a piggery near St Johns Church, in Minley Road backing onto Church Path. In high summer it was only advisable to use this short-cut to church if you were able to hold your breath for at least two minutes. An oddity about Parsonage Farm was in its roof construction. The ceiling joists were only squared on their underside, being half-round roughly trimmed pine poles. This made walking about the roof-space difficult. A massive 'back-to-back' fireplace filled the centre of this old house to the full depth of front and back hallways.

Trunk Farm and **Old Trunk Farm** were divided by the main line railway coming through in the early 1800s. But access along Trunk Lane was maintained by Sexes Bridge. The origin of its name unknown; it was liable to deep flooding so passage on foot was aided by a raised sarsen stone walkway. For some years Trunk House was the home of the Bootle-Wilbraham family, the Colonel was Commander in Chief of the Coldstream Guards and whenever the band played on the wireless it was 'with his kind permission'.

Doglets in Southwood Road was another old farmhouse converted into a gentleman's desirable residence, but still preserving the large open fireplaces and two wells.

Hooks Farm, later Cove Cottage and now called Cranleigh Court. This was a fine and extremely old house dating back before Elizabethan times into the 14th century. Over the years it had been extensively altered and restored; like many houses of those times, the bedroom windows faced south towards the lane, while a long passageway ran the whole length of the north wall. It was this corridor that added to stories about Cove Cottage. There was a considerable inward tilt, that combined with the highly-polished floor made walking difficult, this and a full-length mirror on the far-end wall, started many a ghost story. This passage highlighted another feature of the house's history. At some time the front hall had been heightened by removing a bedroom above so making a lofty dining room. But the top passage could not be cut out, so it was left open with waist-high oak panelling, in time this got called the 'minstrel gallery'.

Throughout the 1920s and 1930s, Cove Cottage was the home of Major Wilson and his family. It was one of the 'big' houses that found work for many Cove villagers; the Wilsons employed a cook and kitchen maid, two housemaids and a garden-boy. For special occasions extra local help could always be called on from the village.

Even the Reverend and Mrs Watson at the Vicarage had two 'live in' servants. They worked long hours for not very high wages, but with some compensations, at least they had their own little sitting-room next to the kitchen. Unfortunately the Vicar's wife was very strict and would on no account tolerate 'friendly visitors'. We all thought it rather unfair when she dismissed one girl at a moment's notice simply for some small and probably perfectly innocent indiscretion with a bandsman at the annual Vicarage Garden Party. Perhaps we did not know the full facts, but I am sure her friend Nellie knew and still keeps her secret.

Whitehall Farm was up Southwood Lane, again away from the village and on ground 'purchased' by the War Department in the mid 1800s. For years it was rented and occupied by the Oakey family to graze their dairy herds. The land was mostly water-meadows, but the 'big field' opposite the farmhouse was larger than any in Cove and in the early 1930s hosted an air-show by Sir Alan Cobham's Flying Circus. This is all in the past and will soon be forgotten for there is not a single farm left in Cove. However the ponds by Whitehall Farm can still be seen by the roundabout at Southwood Road and Ively Road junction. Gone too are the grazing fields, no longer needed for there are no cows, horses or pigs. Soon the last remaining water-meadow in the village by Arrow Road is to be built over.

Chapter Three
Tower Hill

As happened with all of the Cove farms, most of the really old houses that once graced our village have long since disappeared. We still have those faded sepia photographs giving us a picture of how the houses looked from the outside, but there is very little on record to show us the inside. This was all within the memory of many villagers, but it is doubtful whether even the oldest elder citizen can go back beyond the turn of the century. So let us explore Cove's streets and lanes and while doing so take a peep through a few front doors.

Let us begin in Tower Hill, the road between St Christopher's Church and the Queens Head. It is probably one of the original village lanes for even today it has no drains to take away rain water and for most of its length no footpath. It got its name by being close to the first 'Tower Hill'.

The name 'Tower Hill' over the years has moved steadily westwards along the low ridge that is Cove. The original Tower Hill was near the junction of Marrowbrook Lane and Victoria Road just over the parish boundary in Farnborough. Here there is no obvious hill, but if viewed from the old road that ran along the edge of the low ground where Solatrons factory is now, this would have appeared as a high slope, especially if topped by heaps of large stones.

The first school to carry this name was on the corner of Wood Lane and St Christopher's Road. Before 1930 a new school had taken the name of Tower Hill another half mile further west – to a site off Fowler Road in the highest part of Cove.

I am deliberately starting at Tower Hill House because it was the home of my mother's parents, Mr and Mrs John Hill. My grandfather, Mr John Hill, was a market gardener from Wisbech in Lincolnshire who came to Cove nearly a hundred years ago with his wife, two sons and two daughters. He established a family business as nurseryman, florist and landscape gardener. There was plenty of scope for the latter. Farnborough at the turn of the century was a rapidly expanding residential area as Farnborough Park was being divided up and sold in individual one hundred foot frontage building plots.

The old house, known in the 1870s as 'Hill House Pottery', was so marked on the oldest maps. It was surrounded by brick outhouses that had been used for the storage and stacking of finished pottery. Other sheds sheltered the potters whose skills at the shaping and firing of clay pottery made Cove a well-known name in the pottery industry. I think it would be

(Top) Tower Hill House in the first years of the 1900s.
(Bottom) Tower Hill House – demolished in 1972.

correct to claim that the clay for every brick and tile used in this 18th century house and its outbuildings was dug, shaped and 'kilned' within the village of Cove.

The photograph of Tower Hill House, unfortunately marred by a dark line, shows the first greenhouse constructed by my grandfather in the first years of the 1900s. Close by is a small brick building. It was on this spot that recent excavations by a local archaeological society found the workshop floor to be a foot deep in broken and discarded pieces of pottery. The bricks used for the greenhouse were those salvaged from the demolished potters' sheds. Another detail in the photograph that gives an indication of the passage of time, is the large silver birch to the right that must have been cut down soon after this photograph was taken. For to my certain knowledge, a pear tree grew on this same spot; it survived to maturity bearing a yearly crop of small sweet fruit and eventually met the same fate as the silver birch. Had it stood it would be right in the middle of the present road.

The more recent photograph shows Tower Hill House shortly before demolition in 1972. When we compare these two photographs, taken almost a century apart, there is little obvious change in the external brickwork. Thus it might be assumed that the frontage of this 18th century house could have remained unaltered for nearly 250 years; the only additional feature seems to be the glassed-in porch added in about 1910. The windows are a perfect example of continuity with their low curved brick arch above, filled in with a fillet of wood, a single bar across each window and only the centre casement opening. This same feature appeared on other old houses in the village built at about the same time which leads one to suspect they may all have been put up by the same builder and the windows made by the same village carpenter. On the inside of each set of windows was more evidence of skilled woodworking craftsmanship. The polished oak sill was wide enough for comfortable seating and at each end oak panelled cupboards concealed folding wood shutters that closed across the windows at night.

Both views show the massive chimney breasts and what looks like black bricks. These were in fact shiny blue or green glazed bricks reclaimed from the old pottery kilns. The colouring resulted from placing the bricks on the floor of the kiln before loading the freshly glazed pots for firing. The wet glaze dripped down onto the bricks and each time the kiln was dismantled the thrifty old potter put these to one side to build into the outer wall of his new house. The north-facing front side of the house over the intervening years has acquired an insulating coat of ivy. This ivy could only root itself to the right of the front porch at ground level as on the other side were cellar windows.

John Hill & Son – Tower Hill Nursery.

The photograph taken in the early 1900s, a few years after completion of the greenhouse, shows the interior of the greenhouse in full production with plants to exhibition standard. The bearded gentleman in the foreground is my grandfather, John Hill, and the others working in the greenhouse are my grandmother and Edwin Hill known as 'Uncle Ted'. All three are buried in the family grave in St John's churchyard, Cove.

Tower Hill House was demolished in the 1970s. Unfortunately memories are only available from the 1920s, and all interesting structural features have long since been destroyed. When the builders dug footings for Nos 18, 19 & 20 Tower Hill, the present houses that replaced it, they came upon layer on layer of broken rejected red clay pottery pieces. The old house got its revenge as the builders were confronted with buried cellars, cess-pits and long forgotten wells.

The layout of Tower Hill House was similar to many other old Cove dwellings of the 18th and early 19th century. Its roof having two gables like a letter 'M' avoiding the need for long heavy timbers. A good example of this sort of construction can still be seen in the older part of Cove Vicarage (earlier Home Farm and now Penbroke House) with its two small gables and chimneys set into each end. What was unusual about Tower Hill House were the massive oak beams spanning two downstairs ceilings; these overlapped each other by several feet, their ends protruding into adjoining rooms. The colour and texture was like coal, too hard to ever have been sawn or nailed. The cool cellar was reached down winding, worn brick stairs; set into its walls were half-round niches to stand milk and cream.

All drinking water came from the deep well outside the back-door, drawn up in buckets. It was kept in two large earthenware bowls on a trestle table just inside the kitchen door and covered with cheesecloth to keep always cool and fresh. These bowls known as 'bread crocks' were made locally and served many purposes in the kitchen, some have still survived after many years of use. The only memento left from memories of those days, is a round wooden holder that once topped the newel post halfway up the stairs. When darkness fell, this held a lighted candle so as you went to bed, clutching stone hot-water bottle and candlestick, you took your light from it and the last one up 'carried the candle'.

Baggs Cottage stood in a triangular plot of ground where Tower Hill and St Christopher's Road meet. This thatched cottage was demolished early this century when Percy Instone, who owned the garage opposite, built his house, No 1 Tower Hill, over the site of the old cottage. This being prior to the 1914-18 War is beyond my memory, but we have two witnesses both well over 80 who can give a description. My sister Evelyn, who as a small child lived with her grandparents in Tower Hill House, remembers bending low to look in the windows beneath the thatch of Baggs Cottage. Also Bill Chiles, whose father had a grocer's shop in Cove Road, recalls this small cottage and the Baggs family – the last occupants.

How does one estimate the age of this example of our village heritage? There were a few clues left. Firstly as it was alongside the track into Home Farm, it was probably built for a farm labourer. Secondly it was thatched with local Norfolk reeds that grew in the reed-beds alongside what is now Arrow Road, when nearby houses of the 1750s were clay-tiled. The real mystery of Baggs cottage was buried deep beneath its floors. Recent excavation by Mr Jones, the present owner of No 1 Tower Hill, uncovered the centuries-old original foundations. These were huge blocks of sarsen stone, some weighing over 300 pounds. Along the more or less level tops of these large stones, was laid a course of mortar and brickwork forming the old cottage's outer wall. The soft red bricks would almost certainly have been 'Cove made', probably from the clay pits and brick kilns just off Arrow Road.

Sarsen is not a stone normally used by stonemasons, it being difficult to dress. But as it is usually found in its natural state with at least one flat and level surface, it was used many years ago in foundations. Witness the number of nearby old churches built upon huge sarsen stones.

But where did they come from? There have never been large stones found beneath the ground anywhere in Cove, the nearest source is some miles away along the Chobham Ridge. It is feasible that some were 'borrowed' from a prehistoric site on Tower Hill, especially as the stones used in this cottage foundation were obviously 'second-hand'. Some showed signs of being subjected to intense heat, the scorch marks penetrating several inches into the solid stone.

The candle-holder that once lit the stairs in Tower Hill House. One of the few items to survive 250 years of village domestic history. With it is the scissor-shaped candle snuffer used to pinch off the lighted wick.

(*Top*) *Pottery relics from Tower Hill Pottery. A clay tile covered in glaze, a honey-pot, two kiln support rings and a selection of pot handles that failed to 'stick'. (Bottom) The 'little & large' of 'Cove ware': a honey pot in perfect condition although buried for many years; the 'bread crock' was in daily use up to sixty years ago holding fresh well-water.*

(Top) The author with some of the sarsen stones that formed the foundations of the ancient cottage in Tower Hill. (Bottom) The largest stone recovered from beneath No 1 Tower Hill weighed over 380 lb; an even heavier stone was left in situ as it could not be lifted from the trench.

Chapter Four
Old Houses, Shops and Chapels

Prominent premises along Cove's main street include the Methodist Chapel. I cannot remember if the present one is the third or fourth to occupy this site, but like many people I think the first one had more character with its upstairs and downstairs.

Next to the chapel came West End Place, eight adjoining ivy-covered cottages that somehow got the unflattering title 'Bug Row'. Just along the road was the Misses Twitchens Post Office, more recently a shop making and selling plates and crockery. By the 1930s, the Post Office had moved round the corner to its present site at No 5 Bridge Road.

Next to the old Post Office and back a bit off the road was the 'Tin Chapel' built on a triangular plot of ground now occupied by Nos 98 & 100 Cove Road. It was here that we children first enjoyed the simple pleasures of the 'Magic Lantern' and I still remember the hymns that accompanied pictures of 'Greenland's icy mountains' and 'Africa's coral strands'.

Bridge Road, Cove in the early 1930s photographed by Mr Hancock.

At the corner of Cove Road and Bridge Road was the then imposing Hemmings Stores. The photograph shows the view up Bridge Road in the early 1930s. It was taken by Mr Hancock a photographer from Cove Road. His son Reg continued his business from his shop at No 44 Cove Road until retiring a few years ago. The boys in the photograph were coming home from school and seeing Mr Hancock setting up his tripod decided to get in the picture. The lady looking out of her window at No 42 Bridge Road is most likely Mrs Short for she lived in that house at that time.

Some of the 'lads' still live in the village, so I hope they will not be offended by the use of their more familiar names. There are three 'Ronnies', Ron Brown, Ron Lynch and Ron Young, alas these last two are no longer with us. Also there is 'Ginger' Newton, 'Fatty' Legg and another Brown, 'Kitch' named after the famous general of the Great War, Lord Kitchener; the boy in the centre wearing a cloth cap is 'yours truly'. Those were the days when bicycles outnumbered motorcars; there are at least four bikes in the view and only a single car at the top of the hill outside H Silvester's sweet shop on the corner of Highfield Road.

Further along Cove Road on the right, just beyond Cove Brook are a row of 16 small cottages known locally as Nash's Row. When first built they may have had the grander name of Victoria Place after the 'old Queen', but few in the village would recognise that name. For everyone knew they were put up by old Mrs Nash as an investment, the rents provided a steady income for her son 'Neddy', a shy lonely lad who grew up to be a shy lonely man. Nobody in Cove seemed to remember his true name, it was only by pulling brambles and ivy away from the Nash family grave near St Johns Church, that I found he was born in 1908 and named Henry. The houses have stood the test of time, but their gardens have suffered. Originally although each was only 20 feet wide, they stretched back over 200 feet to the small paddock, which, with most of the long gardens disappeared when Nash Close was built.

Beyond West Heath railway bridge, The Plough and Horses pub was originally called The Plough, 'the horses' were added later. It has the familiar double-pitched 'M' roof common to many older Cove houses. A little way up Fernhill Road is April Cottage. This may have once been the Jolly Sailor public house; its front door was on the corner facing what was then Hawley Road. The lane beside the cottage was the back way into Blunden's West Heath Farm. Another drive into the farm started by the West Heath railway bridge.

Any reader sufficiently interested can consult in the Public Library a Drews or Sheldrake street directory for the 1920s and 1930s for a list of shops in Cove. What is more important is getting to know those local people who met or served the folk of Cove. Let us start on the corner at Instone's Garage staffed by Percy Instone himself, Mr Petty and the two

(Top) The Plough and Horses originally called The Plough. Note the familiar double-pitched 'M' roof. (Bottom) April Cottage, Fernhill Road – may have once been the Jolly Sailor public house.

Petty boys, not forgetting Geoff Newman who, although confined to a wheel-chair, was a fine mechanic and would even 'man the pumps'. These hand-operated petrol pumps stood against the pavement, an arm swung out over the footpath to fill cars on the road. Ten cranks of the handle delivered one gallon of National Benzole costing 1/10d (or about 9 pence in modern currency). This may sound cheap, but when a labourer's wage was only 10d an hour (about 4 pence), it is the modern equivalent of nearly £8 a gallon.

Directly across the road from Instones, the Hill family each provided a different service to the community. Mrs Hill had a fish and chip shop why did chips always taste better when eaten out of newspaper? Of course in those days the paper was vinegar-proof and did not smudge your fingers. Hard-up kids could always get 2d worth in exchange for a bundle of outdated newspapers. This one-time 'chippy' was until recently a ladies hairdressers. Next door, where they now sell car engines, 'Sonny Hill' kept a butcher's shop and Mr Hill was also in business on the same premises as a turf accountant.

Thorntons shop – No 1 Bridge Road – is on the corner of Bridge Road and Cove Road; it is now owned and run by Mrs Freda Broome. This is one of the only two shops in Cove still trading under its pre-war name and selling the same line of goods. One of Mr Thornton's weekly advertising

Thorntons' haberdashery and outfitters shop.

THORNTONS' OF COVE
"A PUSH, IN BOOTS."
A man fell down outside our place,
The home of "THORNTONS' BIB-
AND-BRACE."
"What's on!" we said. "Is it a lark?
Your feet have made the shop go dark.
Can you get up? Are you all right?
We thought you'd closed us for the
night."
Shortfellow.

Thorntons' Bib-and-brace poem from the Aldershot News, *1941.*

contributions to the Aldershot News was an amusing little piece of poetry
under the name of 'Shortfellow'; one of his best-selling lines were men's
working overalls 'bib and brace' made by a firm called Bolenium. Another
advertising outlet, long before this new-fangled TV had been invented,
was a radio programme broadcast from Radio Luxembourg entitled
'Bolenium Bill on Morning Parade'.

Next to the 'poet' Mr Thornton, at No 3 Bridge Road, was a
greengrocer's shop kept by Mrs Stubbings, who suffered from a slight
twitch. She was related to Percy Instone the garage owner and George
Instone the village wheelwright. No 5 Bridge Road was and still is Cove
Post Office. It was run then by Mrs Crawford, she was very proud to talk
of her son who was an officer in the Merchant Navy. Next door at No 7
was a Mr J P Cassidy, but no matter how much I rack my brains, I just
cannot remember what he sold.

As you may have guessed, the other shop still trading under the same
name and offering the same service is 'Silvesters' cycle shop opposite Cove
Green. It was here a mere sixty years ago you could get a puncture mended
by Tom Silvester, the present owner's uncle, for 6d – a charge that went
unchanged for 30 years. Today the cost has gone up to £6, this of course
includes a new tube, but it only goes to show how much our money has
been devalued. The shop is now owned and run by Ewen Silvester,
nephew of Tom Silvester.

It is good to think that at least two of the old Cove trade names still survive. Once there were two or three good butchers, Webbs, Haytons and Hills. There were several dairies including Watts, Alan Hammer of West Heath Dairy and Mick Yeomans; more grocery shops than I can remember: Mark Chiles, Gobey's, Mr Watts, Hemmings Stores and of course there was always a Yeomans. In those days almost every other shop sold sweets; now in the village it seems every other shop contains a different house-agent.

Next to Silvesters is the Labour Hall. This hall was one of many 'temporary' buildings erected during the 1914-18 Great War as it was known until the Second World War. Once Cove had dozens of such 'temporary' buildings. The Labour Hall is the only one to survive in its original condition. Many other such temporary buildings have disappeared including the original Tower Hill School made up of two such huts. St Christopher's Church was a building similar to the Labour Hall, it became the Church Hall after the present St Christopher's Church was built before finally being demolished. West Farnborough Club – first known as Cove Institute – was a collection of several huts surrounded by thirty similar huts providing houses for RAE personnel. These huts were demolished just before the 1939-45 War when the present married quarters were built. In Highfield Road, Cove, several 1914-18 huts were made into homes and, due to the care and attention of their owners, you would have difficulty in recognising them as such.

Labour Hall a 'temporary' 1914-18 building still going strong!

Chapter Five
Cove People

The good that some people do makes a lasting memory, especially when we were young and growing up. Everybody will have their own favourite 'unsung heroines', and some may even agree with the Kindly Cove Ladies mentioned here.

Mrs S P Gilderdale was the Headmaster's wife at Cove School. For most of the time her home was surrounded by noisy schoolchildren. One day a small boy dropped his rather grubby hanky; it was handed back to him the next day neatly washed and ironed by this lady who, just by looking-on, knew as much about children as the 'Head'.

Mrs A V Gibson Soote was an elderly gracious lady who lived in Woodlea, a large rambling house in the thickly-wooded grounds between Cove School and the Bowling Green. Before the dark nights of winter set in, the local gasman and his apprentice spent a day cleaning and adjusting the dozens of gas-lights in the house. Her cook/housekeeper had been instructed to ensure an ample supply of steaming hot cocoa and fruit-cake. The work meant taking down and carefully washing dozens of fragile glass globes, with not a single word of reproach from the lady of the house for the occasional inevitable accident, so long as the pieces were swept up.

Still in use during the early 1930s were gas-mantled table lamps with green silk covering outside the glass, known in the trade as 'Anti-Zepp' shades. The intention being to dim the light should the dreaded German Zeppelins ever have the audacity to raid as far inland as Cove.

Aunt Hettie or Mrs Charles Knight lived at No 55 Hawley Road (now known as Fernhill Road). In the days when Andrews Road was still a field stretching between Fernhill Road and Minley Road, schoolboys liked to slide down its grassy banks. One day a small lad failed to notice a broken bottle half-embedded in the ground. It was Aunt Hettie who patched up both schoolboy and torn trousers. When war came in 1939, most lads away from home kept a memento to remember fond ones they had left behind. But there was one local lad who carried a permanent reminder of the grassy banks and green fields of Cove. For page 3 of his AB 64 Pt 11, the soldier's pay-book, under 'Distinctive marks and minor defects' was written 'scar on right buttock'.

Miss 'Sally' Rolls a teacher at Cove School in the 1920s and 1930s, every year would write off to different firms for small items to ensure each child in her class got some sort of Christmas gift.

Closer to home are the memories of our grandmother, **Mrs John Hill**, who lived at Tower Hill House in the early 1920s when it was a nursery, for flowers and plants, not children. A memory recalled by scents and taste, for outside the back-door was a large fragrant rosemary bush from which she made her own brand of 'hair-wash'. I also suspect that when making pastry, she would pinch a sprig in her fingers giving her jam-tarts an uniquely tangy flavour. Grandmother's cakes were without equal; year-after-year she won the 'McDougalls Self Raising Flour' prize at the annual Vicarage Fete. This was quite an achievement and against considerable opposition, for those were the days when no self-respecting Cove family would even think of eating 'shop bought cake'.

There were of course well-known and respected Cove ladies who do not quite qualify for the title of 'kindly'. Like **Mrs Yeomans**, the landlady of the Potters Arms who, back in the 1920s and 1930s, did not insist that her customers bought beer, but was just as content to make a pot of tea to go with a workman's bread and cheese. What memories this brings back of bar billiards, wooden benches and the tap of dominoes on scrubbed tables.

Many will remember **Mrs Jones**, 'Snowball's' mum, who provided a useful community service by running a clothing thrift club long before Grattons or Littlewoods were heard of. Then there was **Mrs Brown**, Rosie's mum, who kept the nearest sweet-shop to Cove School, just under West Heath railway bridge and alongside Wrights the drapers. It is not such a cheery place now, for few people walk under the old bridge and the premises now house a Chinese takeaway and some offices. Another name from the past is **Miss Elliot**, who once lived in Gooden Crescent and, as far as I know, was the first local young lady to become a Cove School teacher. Later a Miss Clark of Busk Crescent also became a school teacher. We must not forget the lady who fulfilled a most important duty in the days before hospital and maternity wards were customary. **Nurse Howie** was the midwife who at one time lived in a house in Marrowbrook Lane that is now next to the entrance to Hinstock Close.

Cove Characters There are some people whose lives hardly touched the village and many who spent their whole time within the cottages and lanes of Cove, also a few who only came to do a job or perform a duty. But here we must be careful not to offend by mentioning names of those still around to read them.

Let us start with an inoffensive wooden seat by the bus stop in Cove Road between The Tradesmans Arms and the Vicarage gate. With this very spot in mind, there was an old lady who every Friday and Saturday evening some 70 years ago, used this pitch to set out her fruit-stall. Her name was Mrs Fenton, her husband Nobby had a fruit round in North Farnborough. They lived in Park Place and, much to the annoyance of neighbours, kept their noisy donkey in a small field at the end of this road.

But Mrs Fenton was not the first to occupy this spot. For here once were the village stocks, perhaps for centuries before some other old lady did good business selling rotten fruit to pelt the wrong-doers. Let us dwell for a moment on this terrible form of punishment. Can you imagine the torture of being locked in the stocks on a blazing hot summer's day within sniffing distance of three pubs.

There was one very occasional visitor to the village by the name of Hoppy Miller. Because he preferred a lonely independent life, it was said he set a bad example. Hoppy, so called as he tended to favour one leg, lived rough on Cove Common. His home was deep in Pyestock Woods. He stayed there in all but the most severe weather, secure in knowing he was just outside Camp limits. General orders for soldiers in Aldershot Garrison, warned that over Pyestock Bridge was 'Out of Bounds'. Such a life becomes understandable when considering the alternatives. In Aldershot, in a common lodging-house like old Shamrock at the top end of Crimea Road, he would have plenty of company for painted on the door of each room, depending on size, was Room 2-4 men, Room 5-6 men.

Five miles away on the other side of Cove and even cheaper, was the 'Spike' at Winchfield as it was known to the 'gentlemen of the road'. At this workhouse, Hoppy would have been expected to do a few hours digging or scrubbing in return for bed and breakfast.

There were a few times each year when Hoppy ventured into Cove, but only as far as Hemmings on the corner of Cove Road and Bridge Road or the Misses Twitchens Post Office in Cove Road. For some reason he was very reluctant to visit Aldershot. In fact it was rumoured that it took four of the biggest and best of the Hampshire Constabulary to coax him into the town against his will. Coming into Cove from the common, he had to pass one of the many public houses, the Potters Arms. Hoppy would limp in, a pint of Mays bitter brewed in Basingstoke appeared on the bar, he would down it and limp out. Not a word was spoken, nor a penny changed hands. That kindly landlady Mrs Yeomans carried on as if nothing had happened. The conversation picked up again, having paused for a few moments to let in a small piece of local memory.

No account of village life would be complete without mention of the 'Yeoman of Cove', a widespread family-name connected with every facet of local affairs. There were Yeomans in farming, pottery, shop-keepers, building merchants and publicans; on church, chapel and parish councils, but most of all in sport.

The photograph taken 75 years ago shows a complete football team all with this same name that took part in a sort of 'Yeomans v The Rest' match one Christmas in the 1920s. This was played in the grounds of the Royal Aircraft Establishment Sports Field, then close to the North Gate, RAE. Proceeds went to raise money for the Cove and Farnborough War Memorial Hospital that opened in June 1921. Many may remember those shown in this old photograph, but what might be of interest would be the list of names, jotted down by someone at the time, of the playing positions and familiar nick-names of those taking part. Unfortunately the writer at the time omitted to record either the result or name the opposing team.

(Top) Potters Arms, Cove Road – externally little-changed since Hoppy Miller's visits. (Bottom) Yeomans' football team, Cove early 1920s – Bert (Tiny); Charlie (Shang); Edgar (Buster); W. (Bluff); A. (Stinie); S. (Curlie); Sid (Dick); Horace (Boke); Joe (Darkie); Jim (Nobbler); Arthur (Dusty); Reserve (Em); Linesman (Alf); Referee (Tom).

Chapter Six
School Days

This subject could fill a book on its own. Anyone interested has only to read those wonderful books by Peter and Iona Opie who, when they lived at the big house on the corner in Liss next to the Blue Bell during the early 1950s, started collecting and listing children's games. These two writers later went on to explaining the seemingly meaningless jingles of children at play, like the one that goes:

'It's raining it's pouring
the old man's snoring
he went to bed and bumped his head
and couldn't get up in the morning'.

As many childish pastimes have remained unaltered since portrayed by Dutch artists some 200 years ago, it might seem best to stick to those games we know were enjoyed by Cove children in the 1920s and 1930s. If in those days, you saw two energetic small boys galloping round Tower Hill School's dusty playground with arms crossed and linked behind their backs, you would know instinctively that they were 'bus-horses' – even though this ironwheeled two-horse form of public transport had long since disappeared from the streets of London. Girls drew squares in the dust or preferably chalked in the road for 'hop-scotch'. The were safe knowing only two or three slow horse and carts would pass by in a day. When not hopping, they were skipping in and out, fast or slow, one rope or two.

Small boys were always running usually behind a hoop, but even the humble hoop came in different grades. The light wooden type, favoured by parents, but considered a bit 'sissy'; the old spokeless bicycle wheel cheap and noisy, but the top model was a four foot spring-steel hoop shaped by Dan Spooner at Victoria Road smithy, the join forged and filed until smoothed and invisible. These metal hoops had pace and control, but if bowled into a kerb at high speed were liable to disappear over a neighbour's fence or hedge.

When we went to the 'big' school, games became more serious and in organised teams. But always it was the children who made and enforced the rules, simple, fair, needing no elaborate equipment or uniforms and certainly having nothing to do with teachers' authority. One game was 'Bung the Barrel' played against the school fence, with almost any number of players. The leader stood back to the fence and the rest packed down in a single row like a rugby scrum. First of the opposition took a flying leap to thump down as far up the line as possible, followed by all the others in turn, preferably concentrating on the weakest back. If the line collapsed they went down again, withstanding the combined assault put the other side 'in'. 'Cut Fat' was a complicated game played in the long-jump pit, an area of raked dirt. Each lad jumping as far as he could, the shortest became 'fat' having to make a 'back' where the longest jumper had landed. All then took one stride and over, success meant 'fat' moved on to the next longest landing, failure became 'fat'.

Simple games and not too rough, but with a terrible fate for breaking the unwritten rules – the 'pig' net. Some boys had acquired one of the nets farmers used to prevent livestock jumping out of an open cart. When hung on the top of the fence posts, filled with a guilty schoolboy and hooked up again, it was absolutely escape-proof. The only hope of salvation was to be missed by the teacher during the next lesson.

In those days boys wore good strong sensible studded boots. This permitted another favourite pastime, hanging on and sliding behind the tail-board of passing horse-drawn vans and carts. This in turn raised a familiar street cry of 'whip behind cabby', and a long whip flicked back to wrap round the 'hanger-on's' bare knees.

All schoolboys were avid collectors of 'fag cards', not so much for their educational value, but more for the games that could be played with them. On rainy days Cove School's damp, stone-floored cloakroom always had a few games going on, 'on tops' or 'knock down'. Both games were played by 'flicking' cards from about six paces towards the wall. In 'on tops', any card covering another won all those thrown. In 'knock down', three cards were stood upright at the angle of the wall and to knock down the last card again won the 'pot'. The card collecting 'bug' got one schoolboy a very odd nickname. There had always been the 'appearance' names like: Ginger, Snowball, Fatty, Titch, and Lofty. But one lad who lived along Fowler Road, somehow acquired the nickname 'Products' Haines, simply for collecting a particular series of cigarette cards 'Products of the Empire' and going round continually asking the same question, "got any Products".

Boys and girls at play were kept well segregated by the whole width of Mr Gilderdale's kitchen garden. Discipline was very strict, the cane frequently in use. Really bad crimes were dealt with by strokes from the Headmaster's extra long and 'swishy' cane. Tidiness was encouraged both in and out of school. Each Friday afternoon, two boys were sent to pick up every scrap of paper along the roadside from the school down to the Railway Bridge. A very important person to schoolchildren lived in St Christopher's Bungalow, this was Mr Appleton the school attendance officer. More than one day off without just cause, and he would be round.

Throughout the school year there were 'special' days, like the annual 'School Treat' and the Fair on Cove Green. All children assembled, lined up and were marched up to the Cove Institute (now West Farnborough

Club) and sat down to tea. Afterwards every child got 2d, an orange and a ticket for a free ride on the 'Galloping Horses' of Billy Matthews steam round-abouts. On Remembrance Day, the whole school stood for a long two minutes silence. Above us on the classroom wall was a large picture of John Cornwall, RN, VC the boy sailor who stayed by his gun until death. We thought of our fathers who had served in, and some who had never returned from a war they said could never happen again. Then there was 'Empire Day' when we sang 'Land of Hope and Glory' and of a 'New Jerusalem'. On the same day there was a distribution of small cash awards for good behaviour and attendance. The origin and founder of this charity was never clear, but with childish irreverence it was referred to as 'Barkers Beer Money'. This was probably just another example of a local charity, like the Cove Fuel Allotments, 'lost' when no longer needed or claimed.

Cove School was nearly involved in a tragedy in 1945 just after the end of the War. A captured German Dornier Do 335 fighter aircraft was being flown from RAE by the Commanding Officer of Experimental Flying when it crashed on Cove School. By great good fortune it was just before the mid-day lunch time break, the children and staff were still in class. A few minutes later and undoubtedly many would have been killed and injured. Unfortunately the pilot was killed and the Headmaster's house attached to the school was destroyed.

Cove School much as it was in pre-war days except for the demolished Headmaster's house (on the left) and a new wing on the right.

29

Chapter Seven
Cove Common

The map of Cove Common shows many of the features described that either disappeared with the expansion of the airfield during the 1939-45 War or are behind the airfield boundary fence. Access to Cove Common from Cove Village was by an ancient track now known as Arrow Road; it crossed the Marrow Brook that still passes through the last water meadow in Cove. Beside Arrow Road is a line of mature oaks that are at least the second generation to have grown beside this ancient track. These oaks were recently threatened by felling, but a protest by over one hundred villagers gained a tree preservation order.

For Cove children, the Common started where the houses ended by the small round pond at the junction of Marrowbrook Lane, Cody Road and the Farm Lane (now Hazel Avenue). It was always here they could sit on the low granite stone wall and plan the day's adventures. Using what is now Arrow Road gave them entrance to nature's vast theme park with unrestricted access to the reservoir and across open ground to far-away places like Caesars Camp, Beacon Hill, Pyestock and a long stretch of the clear clean water of the Basingstoke Canal. Favourite swimming spots were stretches of the canal where the bottom was sandy – like Pyestock; here bathers were harassed by big black tree ants, almost large enough to carry clothes away.

During the long hot summers, children enjoyed playing all over the Common. There were small streams to be dammed and trees to be climbed. Whole plantations of tall bendable pines that adventurous boys could climb and travel through the tree-tops swaying and crossing from one to the next. This practice was frowned upon by the War Department Land Agent, a Mr Pettifor, who lived in those cottages in Ively Road opposite the Kennels; for he was the sworn enemy of all children who played on 'his' common.

Our worst fate was to be 'caught'. So when falling out of a tree right at his feet, I had to weigh-up quickly the chances of a fast get-away through the brambles, his corduroys, gaiters and heavy boots against a schoolboy's standard dress of shorts, no socks and plimsolls. To stay and bluff it out won, falling back on the ploy of all local kids, giving someone else's name and address. But it was a mistake having just fallen out of a tree to expect him to believe he had caught a 'Dicky Bird' from Pinehurst Cottages.

Beside the host of natural wonders to be seen, were many engineering marvels on the edge of Britain's largest experimental aerodrome. Partially

(*Top*) *The line of mature oaks beside Arrow Road.* (*Bottom*) *The Marrow Brook flowing through the last water meadow in Cove. In the distance (far left) is Ball Hill topped by the airfield radar tower.*

hidden in the 'Three Cornered Wood' at the end of Arrow road, was a tall half-round brick wall 50 feet high and more than 6 feet thick. It was built to deflect noise away from the RAE offices and Farnborough Town; unfortunately those living in Rafborough had to put up with the noise that spilt round the ends. Behind this wall wooden propellers were driven by two big Liberty engines that spun the 'props' until they fell to pieces. So we had to endure a high-pitched whine, that went on hour after hour; then suddenly the wood shattered, the engines cut-out and blissful silence was restored. To catch the flying splinters, the whole rig was surrounded by a steel mesh of ex-naval anti-submarine nets.

Another mechanical marvel was housed in the old Army Laundry near to the Reservoir. This was an experimental two-wheeled gyro-car. As children we watched and wondered as the driver placed a short wooden ladder against the side and climbed aboard. Then to show off its capabilities, he drove along the top of a low concrete wall built just outside the workshop.

Cove Common has been the scene of several fatal aircraft accidents. Two in particular attracted worldwide attention. In 1913 Cody and his passenger fell from his aircraft to their deaths at a spot near to the base of Ball Hill. Thirty nine years later John Derry and his observer Tony Richards were killed when his de Haviland DH 110 crashed near to Ively Gate during the SBAC air-show. The aircraft broke up in the air and the engines were carried by their momentum into the air-show spectators causing twenty eight fatalities.

Those Rafborough boys who had jobs in Aldershot and made the early morning cycle-ride across the Common, may well have seen the take-off of a large monoplane piloted by Flt Lt Adams or was it Swain? This flight set up a World Altitude Record for Britain, the pilot wearing a forerunner of today's space-suits.

Cove Reservoir although not too clean was, with its wooden piers and changing shelters, a favourite for bathers. The Army contribution to safety was always to have two men out in a picket boat to rescue anyone in distress. This fine stretch of open water, man-made for a specific purpose, was then used for the enjoyment of local people. It was the larger of two artificial ponds, the other being the Horse Pond near to Caesars Camp. Both were made by the Army to accustom horses to crossing deep water by entering and leaving from large wooden piers on opposite sides of the reservoirs; the distance between Cove Reservoir piers was about two hundred yards.

Cove Reservoir was constructed by deepening a marshy area and enclosing it with a long embankment. It was fed from a small stream on one side and a brick weir at the outlet kept the water level constant. This gave a stretch a water covering 7½ acres which to those brought up on feet and inches, is some 36,000 square yards of clear water, goodness knows what this would be in hectares. The maximum depth of water was from five to six feet. When necessary, the water could be drained to allow for cleaning by opening the penstock into Cove Brook; this reduced the depth to less than two feet and the reservoir to little more than a large muddy puddle.

The 'Rese' provided ample space for other water sports besides swimming. Several London and Surrey model boat clubs held weekend events, racing small power boats attached to a pylon well out in the water. A leading local competitor being a Mr Harris from Woodlands Grove who constructed both model powered boats and aircraft. Some stretches of water were popular with fishermen; most of the west bank having ample rush and weed cover. Of course we must not forget the winter sport of skating in those chilly days of long ago when every pond was covered with thick ice. Cove Reservoir was filled in during the 1939-45 wartime expansion of the airfield and its site lies beneath one of the runways.

Streams All over Cove Common and Laffan's Plain, small streams are now hidden, many were culverted during the wartime expansion of the airfield. They bring water that flows into or under the Basingstoke Canal from the hillside of Caesars Camp, Rushmoor Arena and wide basin of Long Valley. Still visible along the canal is the hastily repaired embankment where, some years ago, the Puckridge Stream rushed into the canal with such force to burst through the opposite towpath and flooded two feet deep across the airfield runway. Before the hole could be plugged, millions of gallons of canal water were lost.

One of the larger streams that wandered across Cove Common and along the edge of Laffan's Plain, started near Wharf Bridge on the main Farnborough Road. It was fed by the overflow of surplus water from the Basingstoke Canal, controlled by a penstock made of heavy wooden boards that could be cranked up or down so maintaining a constant water level in the Canal. This stream ran across the Aldershot Command Golf Course, which in those days extended out as far as Laffan's Plain and included the sandy hill on which the air-show stands are built. Between the common

(Facing) Cove Reservoir and its environs.

Surface area of water 7½ acres. Maximum depth 5 - 6 feet. Distance between piers 200 yards.

Fed from stream in bottom centre. The weir was a brick line overspill to keep a constant water level. Beyond the weir was a drain-off controlled by a 'pen-stock' (a water gate). With this the water level could be lowered to less than 2-feet deep to allow for cleaning.

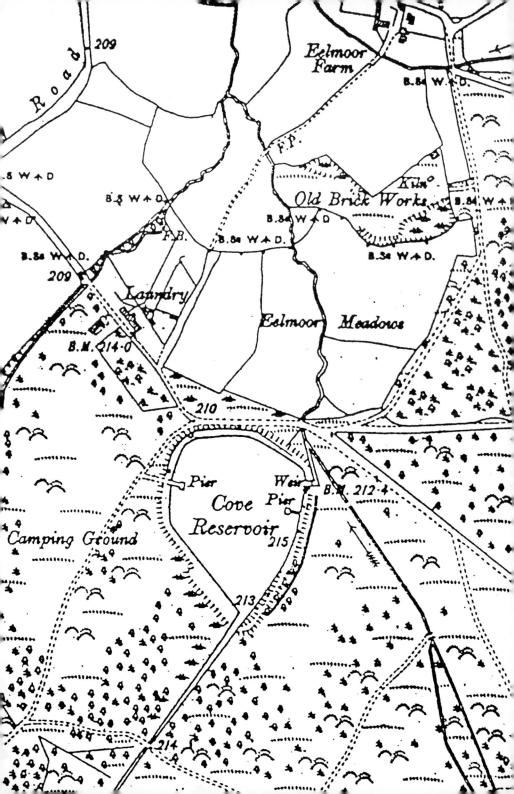

and plain, the stream disappeared through a large concrete pipe coming out several hundred yards away near the end of a road known locally as the Mile Straight. As this stream ran over a clear pebbly bottom, any straying golf balls would wash along the tunnel; so small boys could venture into its dark depth collecting these prized objects. So far on its travels this stream had not got a name; as it turned towards Cove, north of the reservoir and before joining Cove Brook, it became the Laundry Stream, getting its name from the nearby Army Laundry.

When Rushmoor 2000 plans are eventually adopted, an area of Cove Common will be designated a Nature Conservation Area. Cove residents may again see part of the Common that has been hidden behind a barbed wire fence for the past fifty years.

The Mystery of the Disappearing Stones

Many years ago the good people of Cove had certain rights and privileges over the common land that lay to the south of the village. These rights included gathering firewood, grazing their cattle, pigs and other livestock and cutting the turf that kept the cottage fires burning all day and night all through the cold winter.

These old country customs all stopped in the mid 1800s when the War Department took possession of the then common land giving five named Cove villagers with commonable rights a certain sum of money. This was not to buy the land but, as written in old documents, it was to 'extinguish common rights'. So that there could be no argument as to the extent of ownership, the War Department planted huge square blocks of granite at each corner and on any boundary open to question. At the same time these new landowners, upon one day each year, and just to ensure their legal entitlement, denied access to all roads crossing the common.

The map of Cove Reservoir shows in the short distance between Ively Road and Eelmoor Farm there were nine boundary stones. They are designated on the map as B.S W D with a broad arrow marking the boundary. Each stone was enscribed with its number and was within sight of the next, forming a continuous line across country and marking the bounds of Government land that had once been open common.

Now in the whole area there stands only a single marker stone. Boundary Stone W.D No 391, alongside Ively Road where it is joined by Kennels Lane. This solitary reminder of the need in this road to mark the bounds on both verges, for this was not an Army thoroughfare. Even the full power of Whitehall could not lay claim to a right of way that was old when the English Army was still using bows and arrows. For Ively Road follows for a short distance the route of Maulthway, an ancient route coming up from the great plain near Salisbury and leading eventually to London.

(Top) Jack Goddard's Moor, Cove Common – 1935. The small trickle of the stream in the background is the beginning of the Laundry Stream. (Bottom) War Department boundary stone at junction of Ively Road and Kennels Lane.

Ively until recently consisted of two pairs of cottages, Ively Cottages and Peartree Cottages, and Ively Farm. However there were signs that this may have once been a small hamlet for, within a few hundred yards, old maps show several wells and as was usual in those days each well could have supplied more than one dwelling.

Now comes the mystery, why did these heavy granite stones begin to disappear? Familiar stones that had seemed so permanent and solid were uprooted and carted away, no small task for to lift each stone would require at least four exceptionally strong men. Why did the Army decide that the ground they had so jealously guarded for more than a century no longer needed to be marked? Was it in anticipation of 'selling up' or had the 'powers that be' begun to realise that perhaps they had no legal right to occupation?

Although I was only able to find this single stone in the parish of Cove, there may well be others hidden away in the long grass or shrubs well off the beaten track. Should anyone want to go searching, the markers are unmistakable being grey granite, about 12 inches square with two foot of their length above ground and the same distance below out of sight. Chiselled into each stone is the inscription W D and a broad arrow marking the boundary; each bears a number. The widespread distribution of these marker stones becomes obvious from just looking at how they are numbered, for some go well over the thousand mark and of course they once served a very useful purpose. The exact position of each stone being marked on Ordnance Survey maps gave walkers a handy guide to precisely where they were on the open common and heath.

The unwanted granite stones have not been wasted, for the Army put them to good use by lining them up along the side of roads and so preventing vehicular access on to military land. A sad fate for such stones that once had individual identity and a helpful position in the countryside. Perhaps they had served their purpose, for at a convenient height of two feet, the blocks made a hard but comfortable resting place for weary walkers crossing heath or common, but now there being no walkers even this use is no longer needed. These stones too provided a handy mounting-block for tired cavalrymen at their war-games, but again there are no longer any cavalry and the very last Army horses were recently disbanded, there goes another possible use for the stones.

If instead of looking back to the past, we can cast our thoughts forwards a thousand years and imagine what future archaeologists digging in Cove will make of these indestructible blocks of granite. When deciphering the deeply chiselled inscription, what will they think of a generation who had a whole government department devoted to the sole purpose of waging war.

Chapter Eight
Laffan's Plain

On the far side of the southern boundary of Cove Common lies Laffan's Plain, best seen from Eelmoor Bridge over the Basingstoke Canal. Before you, through the high wire fence is not just a featureless airfield, but 100 years of military history. If Aldershot is the home of the British Army, then Laffan's Plain is the wide grassy back yard where the Army learnt to march, ride and later even to fly. It all began back in the 1850s when a military surveyor, Captain R F Laffan of the Royal Engineers, was sent to survey the site for the proposed Aldershot Camp. He saw the grass-covered plain as an ideal exercise area.

In spite of it already having a perfectly good old local name – Jack Goddard's Moor, that a John Goddard was permitted to cut peat on this part of the common in 1750 to 1800, and with many Goddards still living in Cove and Fleet, it somehow got renamed Laffan's Plain. It is still so marked on Ordnance Survey maps. This good captain meanwhile gained promotion, became an MP and finished up as Major General Sir Robert Laffan, KCMG, Governor of Bermuda; but for all his fame his name would be long-forgotten were it not for 'his' plain.

Another nostalgic link between the plain and the Army, comes in the words: 'The song of the Corps of the Royal Engineers'. Once sung, and perhaps it still is, wherever Sappers gathered. It includes the lines: 'We are marching on to Laffan's Plain, where the Old Dun Cow caught fire'. The Dun Cow was a steam traction engine from the nearby Gibraltar Barracks. The chorus names the foreign foe as the Zulu warrior, which would date it to the Zulu Wars of 1879, and featured more recently on film.

Then came the spectacular Royal Reviews, started by Queen Victoria and continued through to the early 1920s for King George V, our Queen's grandfather. I was fortunate as a small boy in 1924 to have seen the last Royal Review on Laffan's Plain. Military historians have written of the Royal Reviews, but little has been said about the Royal Engineers work and planning that made it all possible. This is what the Army now call 'logistics', getting 40,000 marching men on to the Plain, avoiding long dusty roads, by providing shelter and concealment near the parade area.

To achieve this the Royal Engineers constructed a unique system of tree-ringed groves along the southern edge of Laffan's Plain. Firstly by digging a circular ditch and piling the earth inwards to form an embankment on which were planted fast-growing trees. These were familiar local pines interspersed with black Italian poplars, a tree of the

(Top) Laffan's Plain as it was in Victorian times. With the entire parade of thirty to forty thousand troops all on foot or horseback. This would have been the view from the slopes of Puckridge Hill looking towards the present airfield. (Bottom) The same view as it is today taken from what little is left of Puckridge Hill. The same clumps of fir trees fringe the plain, but many have been felled to make space for the main runway and access roads.

fenland and riverbank and completely alien to the sandy heathland of North East Hampshire. When grass-covered with a gravel road through the centre, each circle provided a concealed rest area for hundreds of men and horses and the thinking and planning became apparent. In each sheltered grove different units waited their turn to join the parade; each could form up and emerge to take their allotted place in the line of march. They marched out and round the Plain and back past the saluting base for a smart 'eyes right' to the King on horseback surrounded by his staff of generals. Here on the rise of Puckridge Hill, where a tall flag-staff flew the Royal Standard, stood a smart green and white wooden pavilion sheltering the ladies of the Royal party watching the march-past.

All this is now a memory, pavilion, flag-staff even the hill has gone, bulldozed away to extend the concrete runway. But nature has a way of preserving what men forget and neglect. Down Laffan's Road towards Puckridge Gate, you can still find traces of these purpose-made groves and earthworks. To one side, flooded and overgrown, is a ring of old poplars with its encircling embankment. Opposite behind the perimeter fence, are signs of two similar layouts. There is no mistaking the black Italian poplars, for in photographs of Laffan's Plain they tower above all other trees. As more of these trees die and fall, evidence of these remarkable specially planted groves will exist only in old photographs. At present enough remains to show the original formation as it once was, giving us a living record of Royal Engineer field-works on Cove Common well over a century ago.

Laffan's Road looking towards Eelmoor Bridge. To the left are still traces of the old raised circular earthwork and its ring of tall trees (Italian black poplars) that once hid and gave shelter to troops taking part in the Royal Reviews from the days of Queen Victoria and up to the early 1920s.

Chapter Nine
The Old Tank Road

When in the early 1920s the 2nd Battalion Royal Tank Corps first came to Pinehurst Barracks, they were an immediate success with local children. For from their previous posting in the Middle East, they brought back a pet monkey. We made sure our walks passed the Sergeants' Mess just to see the little chap at his favourite spot on the window sill.

For the next 20 years the Tank Corps were a great asset to life in Cove and Farnborough, setting a high standard in all sports, especially football and boxing. The Corps Sports Day was one of the big events of the year. The Connealy brothers were Olympic class athletes in the pole-vault and throwing the javelin. This in the days when to jump much over 12 feet using an unbending bamboo pole into raked sand was risky. In a javelin throw, one of the brothers managed to pin the calf of a competitor who thought he was well out of range at the far end of the hurdles course. Another sportsman was Private Brennen, boxer and groundsman, who toughened up by punching a kit-bag full of army boots slung from the goal-posts. Cpl Drane excelled in both swimming and diving; for years he was a leading competitor at water-polo having perfected the back-flip into the net and the 'kick off' from a goalies thigh. Having represented the Army and his Regiment so often, he had a shoe-box full of medals to show for it.

Those keen on dancing had top-class music from Sgt Wally Goodman and his band. It is also rumoured that amongst those serving in this camp early in the 1939-45 War, was a Sgt Clarke, Petula's father and also Private Richard Green, who many considered played the most dashing Robin Hood ever portrayed on film. The Sergeants' Mess has become the Farnborough Community Centre and Pinehurst Barracks were close by.

Little remains of those days, Ellis Road preserves the name of an early Officer Commanding and his barracks. But there is still one reminder of the Tank Corps past history not yet completely obliterated. This being the 'Old Tank Road', a test track for these heavy steel-shod vehicles. Immediately after leaving the hard-standing in front of the black tank sheds, the surface deteriorated into a quagmire of deep cloying yellow clay. For this area was once covered by shallow clay-pits that had for years sustained a thriving local pottery industry. This tank road then passed to the north of Cove Reservoir before crossing another wild area. Here were placed vast heaps of tangled and rusty old barbed-wire, a reminder to the tank crews of the terrible battle-fields of a war that had ended barely a decade before.

Within this small mock battle-field were concentrated the whole paraphernalia of trench warfare: tangled barbed-wire, concertina wire, 'A' frames, duck-boards and knife-rests. Each day the tanks churned their way through the history of a past war. Leaving this carnage behind, the tanks emerged to the fresh green fields and gentle slopes of Ball Hill. First they crossed two clear shallow streams, not by bridges, but over tank-jumps made by reinforcing each bank with railway sleepers leaving a 5 foot gap for the tanks to 'jump'. This whole journey as the 'old soldiers' would impress on new recruits, was the motif of the Corps colours: brown, red and green, 'through mud, through blood to the green fields beyond'.

The final part of the Tank Road can still be seen where it crossed in front of Ively Farm, then the Aldershot Command Kennels, and ran parallel with the present Ively Road until reaching Norris Bridge. Once across the Basingstoke Canal and the Fleet-Aldershot Road, the tanks fanned out with the whole sandy expanse of Long Valley to practice over. There is a story which may or may not be true, that a tank-driver when crossing the Fleet-Aldershot road, failed to see a small car driven by the Fleet district nurse and crushed it flat just a few inches in front of her toes.

Tank-jump over stream on Cove Common.

(Top) Ively Road in the 1920s looking down the hill to Norris Bridge. Alongside is the gravel-surfaced rougher Tank Track. (Bottom) Present-day view of tarmaced Ively Road. Little has changed except the line of large-coned pines has been cut down and regrown. The Tank Track is still visible on the left.

When first they came to Pinehurst Barracks, the Tank Corps took over six large corrugated iron sheds that had been occupied throughout the 1914-18 War by the Royal Flying Corps and used as the Southern Aircraft Repair Depot. Each day hundreds of aircraft mechanics, accompanied by their band and with their rolled overalls under their arms, marched down from barracks near the Queens Hotel to work in these sheds. Behind the repair depot was a large railway siding and beyond this in marshy ground were dumped dozens of scrapped aircraft parts, wing and fuselage sections of wood and canvas. A gold-mine for small boys who could make up the flat steel bracing wires into realistic swords and the curved bamboo wing-tip shock absorbers into fine bows.

By 1924 there was little to show of the tank sheds previous use except one old aeroplane that had been left behind forgotten and unwanted. Inquisitive children peering in the gap in the padlocked doors saw a curious blue-nosed aeroplane with canvas-sided cockpits for the crew and open spars down to the tail section.

The Old Tank Road and Ively Cottages.

Chapter Ten
Southwood

Although part of Cove, Southwood is almost a self-contained village in its own right and deserves a history all of its own. The boundaries of 'Southward', as it is named on some old maps, are difficult to define for with the coming of the railway 150 years ago many of the roads were realigned. Travellers from the north, using Trunk Lane, came under Sexes Bridge except in the winter when it was usually flooded. But the mere fact that a low bridge was built in this difficult spot meant Trunk Lane was once an important byway.

Few visible signs remain on which to base a historical past; a field, five cottages and two farms are not much to begin with, but it was a big field, well over 100 acres, by far the biggest in Cove. So lacking ancient remains, let us instead recall past events. For a few days in the early 1930s, the big field was put to a use other than grazing cows for Oakey's Dairy at Whitehall Farm; it played host to Sir Alan Cobham's famous Flying Circus. Crowds flocked to Southwood to watch stunt flying, wing-walking and guess-the-height-of-the-aeroplane. This was when few local people could attend the better-known RAF Display at Hendon, and when Farnborough's only contribution were three oddly-shaped and even more oddly-named flying machines: Gugnunc, Auto-gyro and Pterodactyl.

When war seemed imminent, Southwood Camp was built; the huts were entirely of wood in a 'spider' layout so well remembered by service men and women. This consisted of six 'legs' or sleeping quarters, each holding 30 or 40 beds, depending on the whim of those in authority. The centre section contained what the Army liked to call 'ablutions'. Throughout the war, the camp housed Canadian troops and although called Morval Barracks it was almost universally known as Southwood Camp. Some time after the Canadians went home, the Royal Engineers took over and it became Gibraltar Barracks this name now taken to their new camp at Minley.

Southwood once almost had its own main line railway station; Bramshot Halt, a 'request' stop with 'up' and 'down' platforms, parts of which are still visible by the railway bridge. A station would be appreciated by many 'Southwooders' who now commute daily to Waterloo, but it was closed after a terrible tragedy. When constructing the wooden huts of Southwood Camp, many workers came daily from London, using the 'request stop' facility at Bramshot Halt. Finishing work at 12.30 on a Saturday, there was always a rush to catch the train. This meant a dash up

Southwood Lane and over the bridge to the 'up' platform. There were no staff or ticket checks. Men already on the train would open the far-side doors and urge their workmates to cross the three lines and clamber aboard. Unfortunately, when many of the doors were wide open and men still climbing in, an express came through. These steam engines of the 'King Arthur' class could reach over 100 mph on the 14 mile straight between Basingstoke and Farnborough; so it was all over in a few seconds. The line was strewn with dead and injured and the platforms were never used again.

It would be naive to think that Links Road in Southwood takes its name from the once famous Bramshot Golf Club with their club-house just over the bridge. One fairway ran parallel with the railway lines; a mighty slice could clear all four lines and find the garden of the club captain's house, aptly named The Divots, but it was renamed Bramshot House. In the long hot summers of the 1920s and 1930s, Bramshot Halt really came into its own. For a £1 note, an enthusiastic City golfer bought a return ticket from Waterloo, paid his green-fees, settled with his caddie and still had half-a-crown to lay on the results of the match. The course was not used after the outbreak of war in 1939; the building was then used as an out-station of the RAE until a few years ago.

(Top) Bramshot Golf Club-house that stood directly opposite the railway bridge. (Bottom) Bramshot Halt. Still visible is the faint outline of the wooden platform used as a 'request stop', but closed soon after a tragic accident on the railway line.

Chapter Eleven
Rafborough

afborough is an early example of an estate built exclusively to house workers from one source of employment and all following the same trade. Other such housing existed in the Potteries and at Bourneville near York. But Rafborough was certainly the first development of its kind in the south of England.

Although it has been right on Cove's doorstep for three quarters of a century, there are still villagers who admit they never knew it existed. Perhaps this will arouse a little interest; have those people now living in Keith Lucas Road ever wondered why their houses start numbering from Nos 70 & 71 and what happened to the 'missing' houses. To find an answer, we must go back some 75 years when the Great War meant a rapid expansion in aircraft construction and many skilled tradesmen moved into Farnborough. Most came to work at the 'Factory' or to give its full title, The Royal Aircraft Factory, RAF. So the new estate, built to house these workers and their families became, RAFborough. By 1918, when the War ended, Rafborough was only partially completed. This is why Keith Lucas Road begins at Nos 70-71, the rest of this road was never finished.

In 1918 the Royal Flying Corps outgrew its Corps status and took the title of Royal Air Force. To avoid confusion the Royal Aircraft Factory became the Royal Aircraft Establishment and remained the RAE until recently when a new logo appeared at the Main Gate, it is now the DRA. The present citizens of Rafborough should be thankful that their homes were built in the days of the RAF – the Royal Aircraft Factory. Had this development been completed under today's new regime, it would bear the dubious title of 'Draborough'.

Rafborough roads were given names of pioneers from the early days of flying: Cody, Busk, Weir, Fowler, Gooden and Keith Lucas. The old existing lane already took its name from the nearby Marrow Brook. Many of these names also appear on the Roll of Honour, Farnborough War Memorial, that was once in our Cottage Hospital, but is now proudly displayed in the hall of Knellwood.

When Rafborough was being built, supplies came into a railway siding almost the length of Marrowbrook Lane. Piles of left-over railway sleepers became a playground for children and a welcome firewood for Rafborough families. The estate centred on a School, Church and Social Club, all accommodated in temporary wooden huts. The first Tower Hill School, with its four infants' classes, was in two long huts, but it was replaced in the 1920s by a new building off Fowler Road. St Christopher's Church was in one hut and was replaced in the early 1930s by the present imposing building. Cove Institute, was several huts joined together in almost the same layout as today and now known as West Farnborough Club. The wooden school was built on brick piers and got so cold on winter mornings that ink froze solid in the ink-wells. When no longer used for classes, the hut became a Saturday night cinema, amateurish, silent, black and white, but a great success.

When first built, Rafborough was the very latest in workers' housing development. Each house having three or four bedrooms, gas lighting in every room, a rudimentary coal-fired cooking and hot water system called an Interoven. The kitchen large enough to house not only a sink, gas cooker, mangle and larder, but also a big enamelled bath and a cast iron 'copper' in one corner to heat water for the bath and washing.

The biggest innovation was main drainage. This at a time when most of Cove was still 'slopping out'. A service provided nightly by Mr Marshall's horse-drawn cart, a large iron bucket-like container, which when full could be tipped to deposit its contents over nearby fields. This early attempt at recycling, meant that village children found 'wild' tomatoes plants and grape-vines growing in the most remote and unexpected places.

Public utilities in Cove before the 1930s were dependent on Hartley Wintney Rural District Council, with no sewerage disposal systems in reach. Installed in each new Rafborough house was one of Mr Thomas Crapper's patented, siphonic, flushing water closets, needing proper drainage. So arrangements were made to connect into the Farnborough Urban District Council main drainage system. This scheme was further complicated by the fact that even at its lowest point, Farnborough was some 20 feet above Rafborough. So means had to be found to make water flow uphill. An elaborate system of underground tanks and compressed air pushed the waste water through pipes to join Farnborough's main drainage near Park Place, a road long since buried beneath Queensmead Shopping Centre. The necessary motive force came from the 'Power Station' in Keith Lucas Road. Here were two large Crossley gas engines; belts drove the air compressors that in turn pumped air into the big steel cylinders, ready when needed to push the waste on its way across the fields to Farnborough.

The custodian of these mighty machines was a Mr Leadbeater. Just to approach him at his place of work required an act of courage and nerve. He, being occupationally deaf, sat tipped back in a wooden chair against the far wall behind a newspaper. To gain his attention, one walked between two pounding engines. The wide leather driving belt slapped and writhed less than an arm's length away as it raced off the eight foot diameter polished steel drive wheel to a smaller pulley on the compressor some twelve feet away. Always in mind was the thought of havoc caused in the confined space should a belt break. One job of the local gas-man was periodically to check an unusual device fixed to the wall above these engines. An anti-fluctuator, balancing suction to atmosphere, without which the induction stroke of these powerful engines, would pull in gas with such force as to suck out every Sunday dinner in Keith Lucas Road. At the outbreak of War in 1939, it was realised how disastrous loss of air pressure would be. All waste pipes would fill up and overflow; so to protect against possible bomb damage, the whole building was enclosed to roof level behind a wall of sandbags.

Rafborough once had its own shop; for a few years in the early 1920s, No 154 Marrowbrook Lane was a branch of the Co-op. No 164 Keith Lucas Road was popular with children, for here Mrs Jackson had a table-top sweet counter in her front room. Daily papers: The Star, Evening News or Standard were bought for one penny from Alf or Bill Munday from outside Pinehurst Gate. Sunday papers and our comics were brought round the streets by Mr Anthony helped by young Herbert. Mr Cook had a nearby shop in the then Farm Lane – now Hazel Avenue. His shop had been a two-up and two-down thatched cottage that had been part of Eelmoor Farm. Had this old timbered cottage been restored to its original condition, it would have been a 'gem' of local agricultural history. Mr Cook made a daily round of Rafborough with his patient ex-army mare 'Dutch' pulling his cart loaded with the every-day needs for customers.

We had our moments of excitement as when the hunt came in from off the Common. The fox dived into Jim Bass' garden – No 2 Cody Road, went all through the back gardens between Keith Lucas Road and Marrowbrook Lane, finally to run out pursued by hounds and huntsmen by Pip Turner's at No 1 Weir Avenue.

Living as we did alongside an experimental aerodrome, there were also times of drama and tragedy. As in 1926 when people stood in gardens and doorways watching in horror as a light plane circled, having flown from Brooklands with a man suspended by parachute cords below the plane's tail. Many witnessed this, but nobody seemed to know the outcome. However thanks to Bob Rose remembering being told of this by his father who was working in the RAE at the time, we can now fill in a few more details. The pilot probably decided to make for Farnborough knowing that here was an experienced air accident medical team headed by Dr Saunders. There was probably no communication as this was before air to ground wireless was in common use. Apparently an attempt was made to fly another plane beneath the hanging man hoping to gather him into the open cockpit. What his reactions were to having a spinning propeller a

(Top) Mr James Cook at the doorway of his shop in Hazel Avenue. (Bottom) Jim Cook at the corner of Busk Crescent halfway through his daily round of Rafborough.

few inches below his dangling feet will never be known, for sadly to say he did not survive the eventual landing.

A decade later greater tragedy struck touching all people in Rafborough. On a summer's afternoon one of the new Whitley bombers crashed soon after take-off, no one survived. Among the test crew were two local men, one being Mr Bond of No 160 Marrowbrook Lane. Great sadness also came to the families of two small boys, John Palmer of Busk Crescent and John Williams of Keith Lucas Road. They were drowned when left alone on a bathing float as the crowd rushed away from Cove Reservoir to the scene of the nearby crash.

Seeing Keith Lucas Road as it is today lined with parked cars, brings memories of the days when there were only three motor cars in the whole road. At No 89 Mr Hacker had a Riley Speed Six, Mr Harrison of No 133 a small Morris and at the corner of Gooden Crescent Mark Towers kept his Austin 7. Another vintage vehicle was owned by Mr Hornby in Gooden Crescent, a Scott 'Sociable' based on the racy Scott motorcycle, but fully enclosing both rider and passenger.

Maintenance of law and order was in the capable hands of the 'factory' policeman, Mr Teddy Spriggs, No 30 Gooden Crescent. Although he had lost both hands to an exploding shell in the First World War trenches, just a glimpse of his two shining steel hooks could quell the high spirits of the most destructive young ruffian. Opposite St Christoper's bungalow were the workshops of the Rafborough maintenance team under the supervision of Mr Rossiter; the only other names of his team that still come to mind are Messrs Baggs and Swann.

By 1939, with another war starting and Rafborough 21 years old, many of its boys and girls, also just out of their teens, left to serve King and Country, some never to return. Those lucky ones who came back six years later, now married with children of their own, and, thanks to a caring and thoughtful local council, made their homes in a hundred pre-fabs being built in Cody Road.

The aerial photograph taken in the late 1920s shows a splendid view of Rafborough, Cove Common and the aerodrome. In the immediate foreground are the field footpaths from Cove Common to the centre of Cove Village. All that survives today is the short dogleg path alongside The Tradesmans Arms. Centre bottom is the newly-built Tower Hill Infants' School that has since more than doubled in size as the youthful population of Cove has increased. In the foreground are the three hundred-odd Rafborough houses then only ten years old and still showing their bright shining pebble-dash walls that earned the title 'Moscow' or the 'White City'. Beyond Rafborough and the Marrow Brook water meadows is the embankment of the 'Invincible' railway line as it swings left into the RAE.

In the centre are ten big black sheds that in the First World War housed the then Royal Flying Corps Southern Aircraft Repair Depot. By the time the photograph was taken, the sheds were occupied by the 2nd Batt Royal Tank Corps. Just beyond and to the left of these sheds are two of the original balloon sheds towering to over one hundred feet high. Prominent in the centre is the grass aerodrome with its identifying white chalk circle. An unusual feature is an almost total lack of mechanical objects. High magnification shows what might be two aeroplanes near to the balloon sheds. A cloud of dust along the dirt road in front of the Tank Corps sheds appears to be a 'Lawrence of Arabia' type Rolls Royce armoured car travelling at high speed.

Beyond the grass take off and landing area rises Danger or Cove Hill, its steep sides covered with gorse and its flat top large enough for two cricket pitches and a polo field. At one end is the RAF School of Photography and at the far end is a fairway of the Aldershot Command Golf Club with a green cut into the face of the sand-hill. In the distance beyond the Queens Hotel and Government House, are the Queens Avenue sports grounds. Beyond the rise of Thornhill, if one's eyesight is good enough, you might glimpse the big gas holder in North Lane and in the far distance the long ridge of the Hogs Back.

(Facing) Rafborough, Cove Common and the Aerodrome – an aerial view from the 1920s.

Chapter Twelve
Fords, Bridges, Ponds and Wells

Fords and bridges

The best known and by far the oldest, were two small brick bridges that spanned Cove Brook (once named Dudda's Brook) and the stream that joins it near Eelmoor Farm – the Marrow Brook. For each were built many years ago upstream of even older fords. These bridges have been replaced over the years by larger structures.

The ford beside West Heath Bridge, where Cove Road crosses Cove Brook, continued in use long after the bridge was completed. Horses pulling carts, pulled off and took a well-earned drink of fresh stream water. Steam traction engines rumbled down into the ford to suck up water to replenish their tanks and of course children paddled on the pebbly bottom. The only other bridges over Cove Brook were of narrow wooden planks, one from Hazel Avenue to Ively Road, another between Cove School and Prospect Road across Blundens meadows.

Almost unknown and un-noticed, is the bridge spanning a little stream near the Snow Goose in Fernhill Road, then known as Hawley Road. This stream, which once marked the Cove and South Hawley parish bounds, does not seem to be named, but could be Cove House Brook or Northcote Stream. It starts as an overflow from Hawley Lake. Its flow was controlled by a penstock, an adjustable watergate, where the stream flowed across Bramshot Lane. In 1855 the crossing in Hawley Road is shown as being a ford one foot deep and seven feet wide. A few years later in 1860, the parish elders meeting at the Anchor Inn considered the need to build a bridge. They agreed the water constituted a danger and that the ford was often impassable to the public.

Just as small streams join larger ones, so small fragments of memory join up to make the complete story. So we follow this stream that has no name as it flowed beneath Hawley Road into the meadows where it merges with Cove Brook. Near this junction were a number of black sheds, not enough to make a complete farm, just a collection of pig-sties. These were the only buildings that could be seen from Cove School's extended playing fields that lay beyond the line of toilets and the original gravel playground.

Whilst on the subject of school toilets, I for one cannot face those large blocks of peat they sell at garden centres, without another memory 'flooding back'. A memory that can only be appreciated by boys who attended Cove School in pre-war days and knew what was meant by a 'peat bog'.

But let us get back to the black sheds, for here in the 1920s the dreaded swine fever struck. The agricultural policy at that time being to quarantine the farm, slaughter all animals and bury them on the spot. So hundreds of pigs were killed, a deep pit dug and the carcasses thrown in and covered with quick-lime. It is just a thought, but there might be houses near Hanover Gardens, built upon well-fertilised ground, if located directly above this animal plague pit.

The railway bridges through Cove are unusual for, apart from the new one at West Heath, they all come in two halves, the original brick arches being extended when in 1904 the line was doubled to two up and two down. First built to accommodate horses and carts, the 14 foot width caused chaos whenever two obstinate car drivers met in the middle and refused to give way.

Even narrower is the 80 foot by 5 foot dark little tunnel by the footpath between Southwood Road and Fleet Road. What stories that could tell.

Far grander is the Five Arch Bridge that carries Cove Brook beneath the railway. It was built to take heavy flooding, but its full width is rarely needed these days. It often had to cope with a torrent of flood water 10 feet deep and 100 yards wide, for this is the only gap through two miles of

The original West Heath railway bridge showing the extension when the tracks were doubled from two to four.

railway embankment and it drained a wide area of open common and heath. Cove Brook is fed by many hidden streams. One from beneath the main Farnborough Road ran alongside the Rex Cinema; it now flows under the Police Station and the Community Centre and can still make its presence felt by lifting drain covers after heavy rain. Other streams flowing from the sides of Jersey Brow, carried the dirty waste of the RAE and were required to pass through several filter beds before considered clean enough to enter Cove Brook.

One or two Basingstoke Canal bridges come within Cove. Claycart Bridge near the Golf Club-house is one; here one of the ancient parish boundary markers, the Tichbourne Stone, stood on the far bank. Those familiar with the Common, may remember it as 'Breakstep Bridge', for on an earlier structure was displayed the sign 'Breakstep'. This warned marching troops to break their step when crossing the bridge to avoid damaging the bridge by resonant loads.

Cove Pond

The best known of many ponds in Cove is the one that was once beside Cove Road by Cove Green and carried the village name. It may not have been a natural pond as it was fed by water draining off and from under the road, a road that did not exist before the early 1800s. The water in Cove Pond was maintained at a constant level by a brick over-spill on the opposite side from the road. This overflow water ran off into a ditch, was piped under Prospect Road and down the length of Frog Lane (now called Holly Road). It emptied into Cove Brook having passed under the narrow railway bridge that once joined Cove village with the meadows of Stake Farm and Blundens Farm on the West Heath.

Cove Pond was not exceptionally deep, near the middle it would have been about neck-high to any teenage boy who happened to fall through the ice. Cove Pond gradually disappeared. Not long after the war started in 1939, the drain that fed it was encased in concrete pipes that crossed the pond to a ditch on the opposite side. A series of rare aerial photographs taken from high above the village shows its progress. By 1942 the pipe is clearly visible, half-submerged in water and part of the pond is filled in with tipped earth. A photograph taken in 1948 shows little difference, the area is still wet and the pipe can be seen. By 1954 all water has gone, soil covers most of the pond and pipe. In 1964 no sign remains that Cove Pond ever existed; later the pavilion was built almost over the same spot. The old pond certainly took a long time dying.

Wells

We must not forget that other essential source of water within the village: the well for drinking water and the rain-water butt for all other household purposes. Even as late as the 1940s, there were still scattered cottages lacking the advantages of fresh tap water. Most of the old wells that served for years are now filled in and forgotten. Some were simply covered with a stone slab and left, much to the dismay of later diggers and builders. Two such surprise discoveries have surfaced recently in Tower Hill. A century ago almost every dwelling in the village had its own well by the kitchen door. The 1872 map shows so many in the centre of Cove that they were simply marked 'wells' as a line of dots.

But all wells were not the familiar deep brick-lined shaft; within living memory some folk drew their water from what could best be described as 'well-springs'. In the 1930s the people living in Chapel Cottage and two other families nearby, being beyond the water company's main in Chapel Lane, Hawley, got their water from a shallow well fed by spring water under the bank of a field on the opposite side of the lane. The field is now a school sports ground; the small pool never more than a foot deep and often shared by a friendly frog, has long since dried-up and disappeared.

(Facing) Spring at Chapel Lane, Hawley.

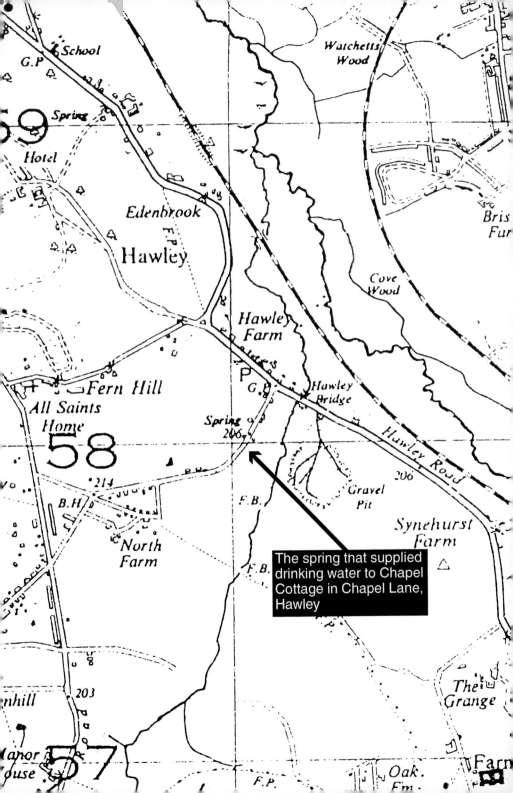

The spring that supplied drinking water to Chapel Cottage in Chapel Lane, Hawley

Chapter Thirteen
Memories of Minley Manor

Although Minley is not strictly part of Cove, so many local men spent a life-time working on the estate during the days of the Currie family, it should be included in our village history. Firstly I must admit to knowing little of the Manor House, its origin, its architectural style, or when or by whom it was first built. All such details have been comprehensively documented by others. But I can claim to have some knowledge of the everyday lives and ways of those local folk who worked in, or around, the Manor and estate.

Such people were on my mind when, at an Open Day and Fete, I stood by the low wall of the South Terrace, picturing Minley as it was back in the 1930s. Through the trees you can just get a glimpse of the Bottom Drive, up which Bill Smith and I, gas-man and apprentice, often pushed our heavy, tool-laden bikes. Opening, and making sure we carefully closed, each gate as we passed through. The Top Drive ran smooth, straight and unimpeded direct to the front of the Manor, without the delays of intervening gates. But this was exclusively for carriages, and definitely out of bounds to tradesmen.

Day-dreaming, and paying little attention to conversation around me, until overhearing a remark that jogged my memory, it being so obviously untrue. Somebody spoke of the view, before shrubs and trees encroached up to the Terrace, saying they could remember when close-cut lawns extended right down to the 'Ha Ha'. Most large country houses have interesting histories, but these sometimes get distorted in retelling, so let me correct one small mistake before it becomes an historical 'fact'. What is now thought to be a 'Ha Ha', an Anglo-Indian name for a concealed wall and ditch, is in fact the brick-lined sunken path from Minley Warren to St Andrews Church. A path that has an interesting history all of its own.

Imagine the gentry looking out over their extensive green acres, with not a house in sight. But there was one small blot on their landscape, a trickle of tiny figures crossing the far lawn, on their way up to church. A simple solution had to be found. So it was decided to lower the path by digging down some six to eight feet, and then lining the bottom and sides with good red bricks. The church-goers, walking up from the Warren, then became invisible from the Manor, and everybody was satisfied.

There must have been some very good reason why so much care was taken to preserve this old path. For in the mid 1800s many of the old rights of way in both Minley and Cove were being closed by the new landowners. Could it have been that this particular access survived because of local belief in ancient Hampshire folk lore. This claims that any path, over which a body has been carried for Christian burial, then became open to the public for all time. There could still be some of those Warren families, with their traditional country names, Smiths, Baker and Chandler, who may recall a funeral when the coffin was carried from Warren to the church up this very path.

So the sunken path remained undisturbed for many years. Until the day the War Department tenant farmer from Home Farm decided to sow barley in the small tree-lined paddock. To gain maximum acreage he ploughed so close to the edge of the sunken path, that he tumbled the whole southern wall down into the bottom of the pathway. There the old bricks have remained for more than forty years. Available should the present owners ever decide to right an old wrong, and restore this possibly unique example of Victorian feudal eccentricity.

On top of the wall by the Minley Hill gate, where the path turns to climb steep brick steps up to the church, you can still see the rusted remains of an old gas lantern. On dark winter evenings, Mr Morris Lunn, the churchwarden, on his way up to open the church, lit the single gas-mantle that shed a faint but welcome light for families following up the dark sunken path to evensong.

Tales have been told, and retold, of life and conditions endured or

The damaged sunken path leading up to St Andrews Church, Minley. The rusty remains of an old gas-lamp can still be seen on top of the brick pillar where the brick steps go up to the road.

enjoyed by those who staffed the big house or worked the extensive grounds. Of estate workers who could dig up fully grown trees, place them on rollers and, pulled by a team of horses, move the trees to a more favoured position. If only I could trace photographs I know were taken at the time. There were some men who spent years of their working lives, on their hands and knees, placing the thousands of small pebbles that form the Church Path, and line miles of roadside gullies from the Manor down to the Lodge gates in Fleet Road. This testimony to skill and patience can still be seen.

Inside the big house, warning notices on the green baize doors between servants quarters and 'above stairs', levied a one penny fine on any unfortunate servant careless enough to leave a door open. A trivial sum these days, but not for a fourteen year old boy or girl just starting 'in service' at two shillings and sixpence a week 'all found'. From all this one might think these landed gentry were hard task-masters. Far from it, Minley in the days of Laurence Currie was an estate of well-stocked farms and sound staff housing. Single men working outdoors in garden or grounds, had their own place to live, the Bothy, built into a sheltered corner of the large, walled kitchen garden.

The Minley cricket team's ground was as good as any in the County, playing host to many first-class sides. Minley Boy Scouts, the 14th Odiham Troop, were the envy of lads from surrounding villages, with their splendid meeting place, the Sybil Hut, donated by and named after one of the Currie ladies. The scouts also had their own brass band, instruments by courtesy of Mr Laurence Currie. They must have numbered amongst the first scouts in Hampshire, for their scout-master, Mr Morris Lunn, often spoke of taking his troop to camp on Brownsea Island, organised by the movement's founder Lord Baden Powell.

Much has been written of those 'to the manor born', so let us instead look at one of the ordinary families whose lives touched Minley. This is the family of George Lunn, born 1857; a labourer when Minley Manor was first built; married when 21 to Ellen Ewins, aged 19, at Mattingley Parish Church on the 18 April 1878. They had four children: George born in 1880, at Mill Cottage, Cove Road, Fleet, as was Arthur in 1882. Next came Morris in 1883. The only daughter in the family was Jeanetta, born in 1885.

When the boys were of school age, the family lived in Farnborough Street and all three boys attended the Old School, near the Forge in Rectory Road. A few years later their father, George, was landlord of the Crown and Cushion in Lower Minley and the three boys, all with good singing voices, were often called upon to entertain, providing their own 'backing' on mouth-organ and jews harp. Plenty of family tales have come down from those days. How grandfather would sober up cavalry troopers from Aldershot by sticking their heads under the pump at the horse-trough by the end wall. How each year, he carefully clipped the yew bush outside the front door to maintain the shape of a crown and cushion. There were also strange tales of hauntings, but then every old house must have its own ghost.

The census of 1891 makes interesting reading, listing as it does the occupants of the old pub at that time.

George Lunn. Head of family. Age 32. Builder and publican. Ellen: Wife age 29. Children: George G age 10, Arthur E age 8, Morris age 7 & Jeanetta F age 5. Boarders: Francis King aged 26 gardener & Edward W Davis aged 26 gardener. It is not surprising that in the census most men are entered as agricultural labourers or gardeners, for all of the Minley estate was then being landscaped. The four children would have made the long daily walk down to the new school that had just been built in Cove and when old enough the boys started work.

The eldest boy, George, married Beatrice and they had one daughter 'Maggie' who lived along Nash's Row. He became a carpenter on the estate. Although weakened when an early appendix operation went seriously wrong, he still followed his trade of carpenter, until the bitterly cold winter of 1946 when he died at his work in Minley woods. Arthur, 1882-1971, went to work at the village bakery at Swallowfield. Often rather than face the long walk home, he would sleep in the warm bake-house on a pile of flour sacks. When 15½ he became a boy sailor on the St Vincent in Portsmouth, a six-decked sailing training ship. Later he worked at the RAE.

Morris always lived at Minley and started work at 14 for Mr Laurence Currie. When the Manor was eventually sold to the Army, he was Clerk of the Estate Office, and the incoming owners found his extensive local knowledge very useful. When he died he had been a churchwarden for well over forty years of the small church in the Manor grounds. He was buried on St Andrews Day, 30 November 1973. His grave is close to the south door of the same-named St Andrews Church, which he had tended all those years. Tributes were paid by one of the few surviving Curries, Miss Daphne, who wrote that "St Andrews Church was Morris Lunn". The Vicar of Hawley described him as "A good man, and full of faith"; a sentiment shared by all who knew him.

The daughter, Jeanetta, 1888-1966, was widowed when her husband, Charles Knight, was killed in the trenches during the 1914-18 War. Her two sons, Don and Ken, spent all their lives in Cove and are well-known throughout the village. Mother was remembered in Nash's Row as 'Granny' Lunn.

Memories and family matters must not deter from the whole purpose of this story, which is to draw attention to the sorry plight of this unusual, if

(Top) Schoolmaster and pupils of the 'Old School' in Rectory Road, Farnborough taken about 1887/8. The two boys in 'Eton collars' to the right of the front row are George and Arthur Lunn. (Bottom) The 'Lunns' at the Crown and Cushion, Minley when their father George was landlord. From left to right are: Jeanetta, young George, Morris, Arthur and Mother.

not unique, relic of Victorian landscape gardening. Can there be anywhere else in Hampshire where so much effort was put into protecting a small community's right of way? Surely this brick-lined sunken path deserves recognition as a 'Work of Historic Interest' worthy of preservation, especially if it could be restored to its original construction and use.

Chapter Fourteen
The Old M Way

Many years before the present M3 cut its wide swathe across the green and pleasant Hampshire countryside, there existed a similar 'M' way going in roughly the same direction and serving the same purpose. The old road avoided town and village, went straight and where possible kept to high ground; as does the motorway. Each is named by the traffic it carried; the modern motorway and the ancient Maulthway, 'maulth' being a Welsh name for sheep.

For this was one of the ancient track-ways, later adopted as a drove road, that criss-crossed the English countryside long before the Roman invaders built their stone paved straight roads. If we concern ourselves only with that part of the Maulthway that came through our small corner of North East Hampshire, we will not have to dwell on where the drovers and their flocks came from, or where they eventually finished up. Our drove, the Maulthway, begins at Well on the North Hampshire Weald; that high ground above Alton, Petersfield and Basingstoke which is also the meeting place of several other ancient track-ways.

Did these flocks and shepherds come all the way from the far-distant Black Mountains of Wales or from the vast grassy plains of Salisbury or Marlborough? Did they make their slow journey along the Harroway coming up on to the high ground just south of Basingstoke, or on the Lunway coming up by Wield on the opposite side, but directly in line with our Maulthway? Judging by the number of important track-ways that terminate on, or cross this area, it must have once been a centre of rural activity. Then came other means of moving large flocks of sheep or cattle, and many of the villages upon the high ground were deserted and 'lost' in all but name.

We can retrace the route taken by the old drovers for most natural features remain in place. The Maulthway leaves the Harroway by the Chequers Inn at the hamlet of Well on the high ground between Farnham and Basingstoke and heads towards London. It comes down the hillside along an old sunken lane and emerges below Horsdon, or Horsedown Common and passes Swanthorpe Farm. The contours have not altered over the years, but the area was then probably more wooded. Then they carefully avoided the two villages of Crondall and Crookham by keeping halfway between them by using the Bowling Alley that now passes The Horns. The route then followed what is now a busy road past The Wyvern, Crookham Cross Roads roundabout and the Foresters Inn. The

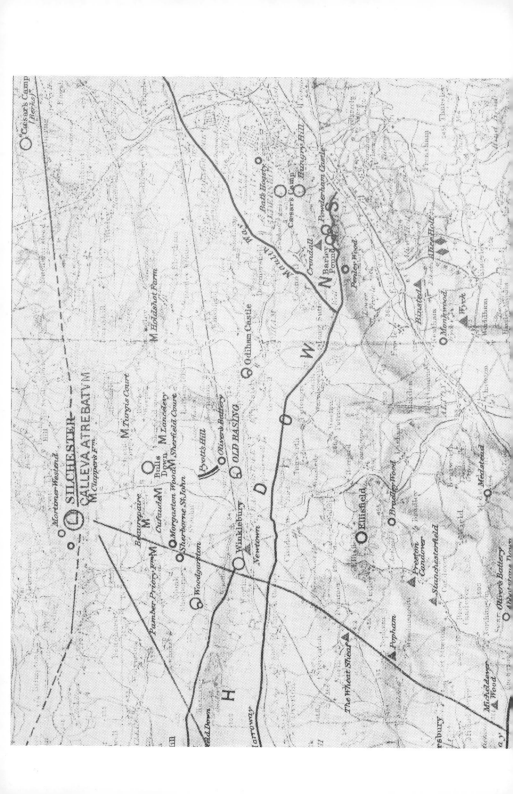

(Top) The Maulthway leaves the Harroway at the hamlet of Well and heads towards London. (Facing) The route of the Maulthway or Sheepway.

number of inns in relatively isolated places bears witness to this being an important route. In drovers' times, the route crossed open country to Norris Hill near to the spot where three parishes meet and, before the Basingstoke Canal was dug, this brought them out onto the wide grassy expanse of Eel Moor and Cove Common.

Here shepherds and flock rested up for the night knowing full well that the hardest part of their long drive was yet to come. Cove Common with its gentle hills on one side and clear streams on the other provided ideal conditions for containing thousands of tired and hungry sheep overnight. So once settled the flocks could safely be left to graze watched by a lad and a couple of ever alert sheepdogs. Whilst the drovers walked down the lane by the clay pits, over the little brick bridge that spanned the Marrow Brook and across the fields to the village and its ale-houses. This lane from the Common into Cove, unaltered for almost one thousand years, is lined by oaks hundreds of years old that in turn had grown from the acorns of previous oaks standing by the same lane. It is nature's link from Cove to the old drove and all the way back to the Great Plain. This lane is now called Arrow Road.

There are several pointers that give us a clue to Cove being an 'M Way' service station several centuries before such things were even thought of.

(Top) The Maulthway passes beside Horsedown along this old sunken lane, a scene that could have been unaltered for hundreds of years. (Bottom) View of Horsedown as the Maulthway emerges from the sunken lane by Swanthorpe Farm, Crondall.

Firstly the number of pubs was far more than warranted by a farming community of little more than a hundred families. Surrounding fields were planted for hop-growing; there were two round drying kilns in the yard of Home Farm behind The Tradesmans Arms. Quite a little industry for a small village with no through road and not even a weekly market. An odd thing about Cove's footpaths is that they all come into the centre of the village from the south or south-west, from the Common or the West Heath. It is just as if Cove never welcomed or expected visitors from any other direction.

Not that these Welsh drovers came to Cove solely to sample the strong local brew. There were more serious subjects to be talked over. Like the conditions that would face them on the following day's drive. Whether to make for the Cole Ford on the Blackwater crossing, or if proved too deep, go a mile upstream to the gravel bottomed Lynch Ford. These river crossings were hazardous at the best of times; for only 150 years ago Lynch Ford was listed as being two feet deep and thirty feet wide.

In Cove there were pottery carters who frequently carried their strawpacked loads to the big city and so got to know every inch of the journey. The shepherds knew full well that at first light they would have to rouse their flocks, go up Jersey Brow by Jersey Farm, cross the old turnpike road by the Tumble Down Dick Inn, down Rectory Road and across Cole Ford into Surrey. Once over the Blackwater, they faced the steep sandy finger-like valleys up onto the wild and desolate Bagshot Heath. Whilst at the village inn, the drovers may well have recruited a couple of sturdy local lads for the passage across this lonely and dangerous heath. For here the 'natives' could appear unfriendly and were known to have scant respect for the property of others.

Being 'Ampshire' folk, perhaps we should not concern ourselves too much with Surrey affairs. So this tale only hazards a guess at those conditions our long-travelled drovers might have faced once across the county boundary. It would be fair assumption that these countrymen did not drive their large flocks right into the London market place, with its toll bridges and narrow crowded streets. More likely they crossed the sparse heathland as quickly as possible and headed for the lush Thames-side watermeadows by Runnymede. Here the sheep could be fed and fattened, later to be 'barged' down to Spitalfields when the market was ready and the price right. We should be thankful to our neighbouring county, for it is they who have preserved the green road's old original title of The Maultway now part of a busy road over the border in Surrey where it joins up with the main road to London.

There is very little history written of this ancient track-way that probably pre-dates both Saxon and Roman times. One noticeable thing about its route is how often it coincides with the line of parish boundaries.

This may have been to avoid dispute on either side, but it could also have been that travellers kept well away from even the slightest hint of civilisation. When the Saxon villagers came to mark their parishes, a convenient and mutual meeting point would be the old track-way half-way between each small village.

What is not clear is whether the same team of drovers made the whole long trek from the far Black Mountains of Wales. Or did Hampshire men, from the 'sheep villages' above Alton or Basingstoke, take over for the final few miles? Did the Welshmen walk back home over the same ground. Stopping off again at Cove and pausing at the Weald villages to talk 'sheep' with the wise and knowing Hampshire shepherds making plans for the next drive.

There is a tale of a Welsh shepherd's means of getting much-needed money back to his far-away wife and children. Knowing how anxious his wife and family would be for money and news, he had trained his most trusted sheepdog to make her way straight back home to their Welsh hill-farm. With a few precious gold sovereigns in a small leather pouch attached to her collar, on his word of command, she would be off and in less than two days arrive safely back home well before any stagecoach over the same route.

This then is how centuries ago Cove village may have played its part in our rural history and why Cove Common covered an area far larger than the village itself. Today if you stand on Cove Hill you will only see the grandstands preparing for the Air Display and acres of oil-stained concrete. But picture if you can this same scene 150 years ago. The hillside and plain a sea of grass, for the pines and yellow gorse only came later with the Army's neglect. Those old commoners would have soon grubbed out such intruders.

Those days can never return, but when deciding between airfield or houses, think of what might have been had this remained common land. See the Common as it would have looked to these shepherds watching their flocks by night from the grassy hillside. When by dawn's early light, the valley would appear to be strewn with thousands of dull grey boulders. It is not surprising that the many sarsen stones scattered around Cove were once known as 'grey whethers' looking as they did like sleeping sheep.

The only surviving sign of 'The Maultway', now part of a busy road on the edge of Bagshot Heath.

Chapter Fifteen
The Old Roads of Cove Village

To understand fully the reasoning behind these thoughts on the ancient track-ways of Cove, you must first look at the roads as they are today. Study these old maps, go out and see the direction taken by roads that still exist today. Take a compass and confirm their lines, and if really keen get up at sunrise on 22 December and see for yourself if the Sun really does rise from the end of Frog Lane (now called Holly Road).

For the more ambitious, I would suggest gaining access to the highest point of the Royal Engineers Gibraltar Barracks at Minley. These barracks are built on what was once the Minley cricket ground. Close by and beside the bridleway and Blackwater Lodge, is a Bronze Age bell barrow at Ordnance Survey map reference SU 828 586. From this point looking towards sunrise on the shortest day (22 December), your line of sight will pass exactly through three other prehistoric markers.

The first marker, now inaccessible, is a large standing (but now recumbent) sarsen stone, map reference SU 848 568. It lies alongside the busy M3 motorway at the base of the embankment behind the boundary fence and adjacent to houses in Mole Close. It is a mystery why a single marker was ever raised in this once wild and empty space on West Heath and how it has survived many hundreds of years of farming, building and road construction.

Next the line passes straight across Tower Hill and the largest known accumulation of sarsen stones at map reference SU 863 555. In the early 1800s these sarsen stones would have lain in open ground on Tower Hill. After 'New Road', later Victoria Road was built, the sarsen stones were scattered around the garden of a house in Victoria Road and many were built into the front-garden wall. Finally on high ground beside Albert Road, Farnborough is another Bronze Age bowl barrow at map reference SU 873 546.

All four of these prehistoric clues to the origin of Cove village are in a dead straight line pointing to the rising sun on a certain day of the year.

Look closely at the maps of Cove village dating from 1750 to 1872 and you will see that little has altered in the last 250 years. There are four roads that concern us, and for each map they will be mentioned in the same order and are far as possible by the name we know them today.

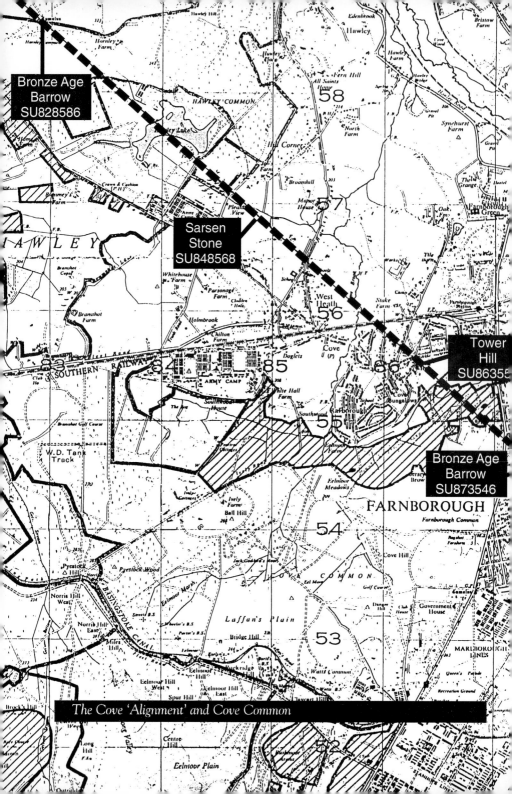

Bronze Age Barrow SU828586

Sarsen Stone SU848568

Tower Hill SU8635S

Bronze Age Barrow SU873546

The Cove 'Alignment' and Cove Common

(Top) Bronze Age barrow by bridleway to north of Gibraltar Barracks, Minley Map Reference SU 828 586. (Bottom) Bronze Age barrow by Albert Road, Farnborough Map Reference SU 873 546.

Map No. 1 is dated about 1750.
First Victoria Road turned south and joined Marrowbrook Lane at the bottom of Tower Hill. The road that passes the Queens Head is shown, but this only leads to an 'empty' area. This road may once have been known as Lion Lane. Thirdly there is another short road, this appears to run directly into the centre of Cove Village and is indicated by the line of houses. Like the previous road, it again leads to the same 'empty' area. Finally Frog Lane is on the map, but its alignment may not be correct; see the up-to-date maps for its possible original line.

Map No. 2 is dated 1826.
Victoria Road still turns south to join Marrowbrook Lane, but now a new road is shown going towards the centre of Cove village. The road passing the Queens Head (Lion Lane) is clearly shown as ending at the parish boundary between Farnborough and Cove. The dotted line shows the boundary between the former Farnborough Urban District and the Hartley Wintney Rural District (that until the mid 1930s included Cove parish). This point can still be found, for the council houses built in the mid 1930s by the Farnborough Urban District Council were right up to the boundary. The short road could have been the village's main street; it was lined with houses in the early 1800s, again this short length of road ends at the parish boundary. If we assume both roads pre-date the introduction of a local parish system, then the ends of each road would have provided convenient 'bounds' marks.

Here then is the first mysteries of the old roads of Cove village. Why did these tracks all finish at the boundary between two parishes? One of the reasons for making roads was to join communities and to provide for easy access between villages. Yet here we have three out of four known tracks all leading to or avoiding an empty space. Frog Lane is still shown, but its true line and direction might not be certain until appearing on the 1872 map, this later map would be one of the first made with modern surveying instruments.

Map No. 3 is dated 1855.
The road shown on the previous maps, running from Victoria Road to Marrowbrook Lane has gone. The short road passing the Queens Head is now extended from its previous ending at the parish boundary, and joins New Road (Victoria Road) opposite Green's School Lane. The 'Main Street' of Cove still appears running parallel with New Road. Frog Lane, now with its direction clearly marked, this probably being the first of these maps made with the help of surveying instruments.

Map No. 4 is dated 1872.
New Road, an extension of Victoria Road is clearly defined and now
named Cove Road. But our previous 'Main Street' has disappeared, the
only clue to its existence being a line of old cottages and several wells.
This line of buildings between junction of Prospect and Cove Roads,
extended as far as the newer parts of 'Queens Head Road'. Several of these
cottages were still there until the early 1930s. Frog Lane now with its line
and direction is clearly marked. Another inexplicable feature of these old
roads is the compass bearing when applied to each of them; because of
this, they could be called the 'Cove Alignments'.

Map No. 5 shows that if the alignment of three roads: Frog Lane, the
earlier Cove 'Main Street' and Lion Lane (passing the Queens Head) are
continued, they converge exactly at the original positioning of Tower Hill.
By a strange coincidence this also happens to be the place where seven
hundred old sarsen stones are gathered in one garden.

Frog Lane is on a bearing of 130 degrees towards the south-east, facing
sunrise on 22 December, the Winter Solstice or the shortest day. If this
line is extended for several miles in each direction, as noted at the start of
the chapter, it passes through two tumuli and a large sarsen marker stone
on West Heath. These three relics of prehistory might well have served as
solstitial markers.

Lion Lane the original short road passing the Queens Head, is on a
bearing of 50 degrees north-east facing sunrise on the longest day of the
year, 21 June.

The 'lost' Main Street once the centre of Cove Village, exactly bisects
the other two tracks, so would coincide with Spring and Autumn
Equinoxes, 21 March and 22 September, when day and night are of equal
length.

So now our old roads, tracks or processional ways, have a purpose. They
focus on one particular place which is no longer an 'empty area'. For here
can still be found hundreds of large sarsen stones, enough to convince
early map-makers that they had found the ancient ruined tower which
gave its name to Tower Hill. We no longer expect to find any sign of a
tower on Tower Hill. In fact it is doubtful if there ever was a tower as
such, for no mention is made of one in recorded history going back to the
Domesday Book and beyond.

It may have been the remains of a circle of prehistoric stones that early
map-makers found on this low hill and then assumed it to be a partly
demolished tower. The sarsen stones as they exist today, although
scattered and re-used, are consistent with the construction of a circular
wall faced with large stones and in-filled with smaller ones. Slab-like
blocks could have framed openings and formed lintels. Every stone is of

the same texture and consistency as one would expect if they all came from the same source. This is most likely to be the Chobham Ridges rather than the far-distant but better known out-crops on the Marlborough Downs or the Great Plains of Wiltshire.

There are those who study 'ley lines', straight lines across miles of countryside that join such prominent features as churches, hill tops and ancient monuments. However the line through Cove is not fanciful. It goes through three identified prehistoric sites mentioned at the beginning of this chapter: two Bronze Age tumuli or barrows and a standing sarsen stone (now recumbent). Also it passes through an accumulation of sarsen stones on Tower Hill. The line points directly at the rising Sun at dawn on the shortest day of the year and is often to be found in ancient monuments dedicated to sun-worship.

Fortunately records have been made by the Society of Antiquaries of London as part of a survey of sarsen stones throughout Wessex. The records are now deposited in Burlington House and of course it refers to 'our' recumbent stone. Other details of the stone and of the two barrows that make up our 'ley' line are published in Hampshire Treasures Volume 3 by the Planning and Community Section of Hampshire County Council.

Perhaps it is fortunate that 'our' sarsen stone is in an inaccessible position, for such relics have a habit of disappearing. A fact borne out by another index card that tells of three sarsen stones near Aldershot Parish Church that were sold to a person in the USA for £60!

Over seven hundred sarsen stones of differing shapes and sizes in the front wall and garden of No 134 Victoria Road, Farnborough.

Map No. 1 – Cove Village, 1750.

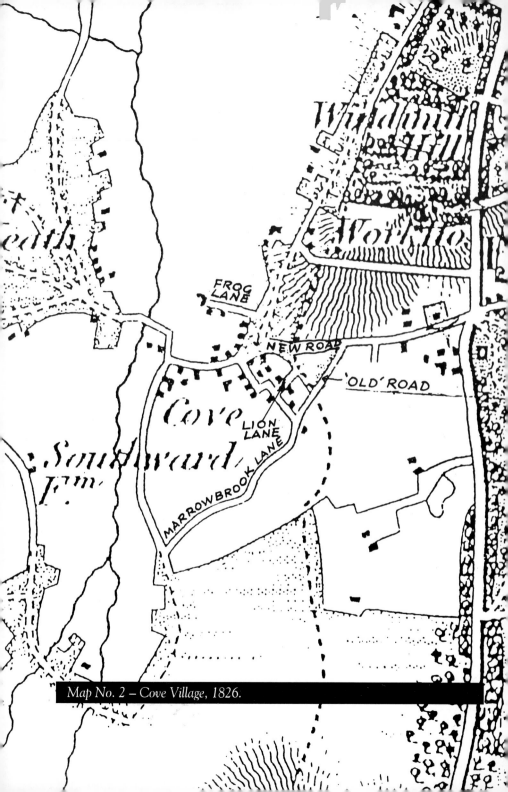

Map No. 2 – Cove Village, 1826.

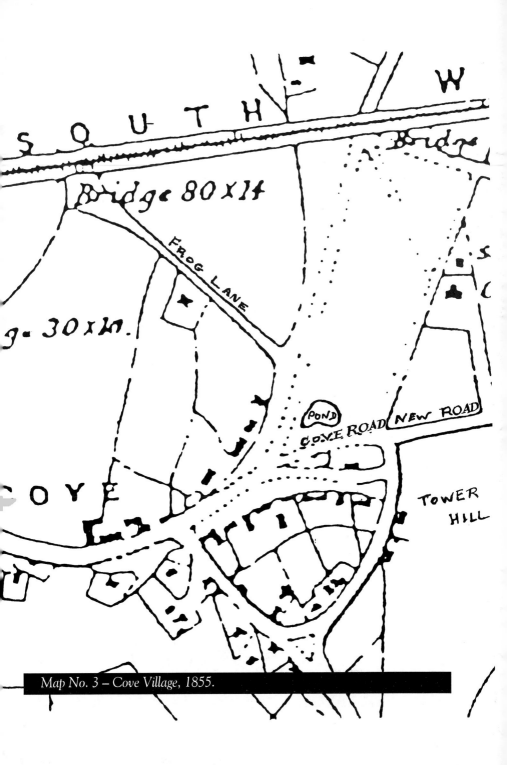

Map No. 3 – Cove Village, 1855.

Map No. 4 – Cove Village, 1872.

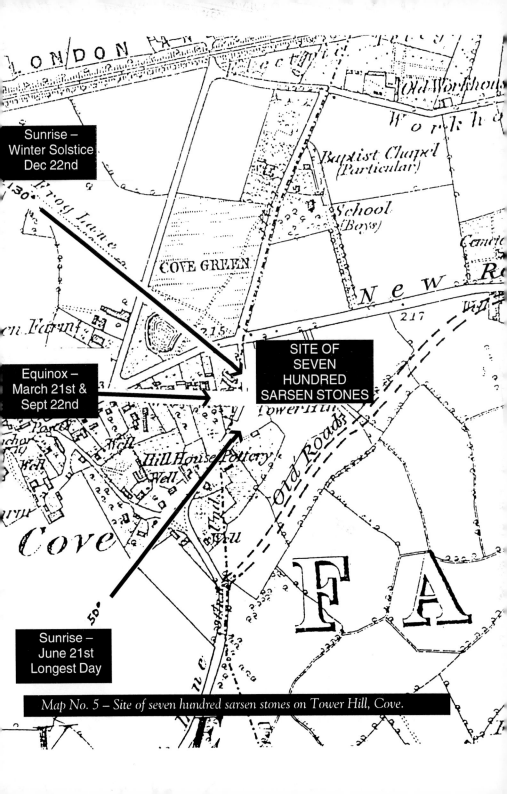

**Sunrise –
Winter Solstice
Dec 22nd**

**Equinox –
March 21st &
Sept 22nd**

**SITE OF
SEVEN
HUNDRED
SARSEN STONES**

**Sunrise –
June 21st
Longest Day**

Map No. 5 – Site of seven hundred sarsen stones on Tower Hill, Cove.

(Top) This may have been 'Lion Lane' in the early 1800s when it ended at the parish boundary by the second telegraph pole on the right. (Bottom) Cove Road and Victoria Road (s seen did not exist before the mid 1800s. One hundred and fifty years ago the original road crossed beyond the big oak tree.

Chapter Sixteen
Prehistoric Cove?

How far can we go back in the life of our village? This is an attempt, supported by a few very solid facts and a lot of imagination, to record one theory of what Cove might have been like many thousands of years ago.

What sort of people were the first to settle in this small North East Hampshire village? Where did they come from and why did they stay? It could well be that they were driven south, man and beast, hunter and hunted, by the relentless cold. For a mini ice age had descended on Britain, with each day seeing less and less of a shaded and feeble sun. Almost two thousand years before the birth of Christ, a large part of Iceland had blown into the sky. For years after, thick clouds of volcanic dust encircled the Northern Hemisphere blocking out the Sun and chilling the air. Hunger drove the wildlife southward and man followed. The animals had an instinct for the old migratory trails that had once led to warm seas and hot countries. But man realised that a few thousand years before the angry seas had burst through the soft chalk downland that once joined us to the Continent, making Britain into an island and cutting forever the tracks that followed the Sun southwards.

Scattered groups of these small dark hunters moved further and further south, down the whole length of Britain, through forest and over frozen rivers. They were seeking a place that would provide their few simple needs. The trees they held sacred, the stones that would help rebuild the hallowed circles, and so restore their once powerful deity, the Sun. Having crossed miles of stony ground studded with pines and birch, they came to the edge of a very wide flat valley. The steep slopes above which they stood were strewn with large sarsen stones. Although the valley was surrounded by pine-topped ridges, within it they could see the oak groves so essential to their pagan worship. They crossed one more river of cold black water and, where the grey stony ground changed to rich dark soil, they came to a low flat hill surrounded on three sides by streams and marshlands and accessible by only a single track.

Here these early travellers found the tall rushes and hazel coppices needed to build shelters, and the oak and beech glades that would feed wildlife through both summer and winter. Nearby was the soft yellow clay they could shape into pots. Their first task was to restore their Sun God to his former strength and warmth. Going back to the stony ridge, they dragged and carried the heavy sarsen blocks to build their 'COVE', a place

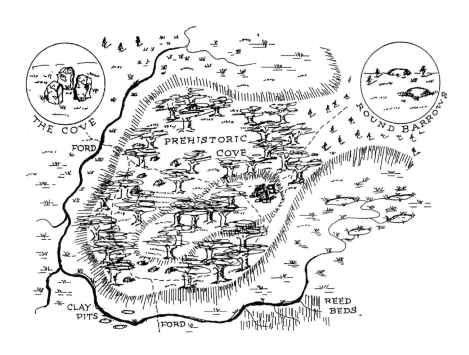

(Top) Prehistoric Cove? (Bottom) Prehistoric 'Cove' on our Tower Hill?

of worship. The wise men laid out the lines and marked entrances through which the rising Sun would enter on the longest and shortest days of the year. These prehistoric cove builders would have picked out a far hill-top or giant oak over which, for a few days each year, the Sun paused in its travel before turning back on its long journey into winter. Such lines were marked and remembered, for they formed the focus of a pagan religion and yearly calendar. For a primitive people with no means of measuring the passage of time, these stone circles were a place of worship, a meeting place and a record of the seasons.

Now after thousands of years, what signs can we still see that were left behind by these early settlers who had no written and few spoken words? How long did they live near their Cove? Was it they who buried their dead in round barrows on surrounding hills? And when the Sun was fully restored, did they go north again or did they remain here in Cove as ancestors to occupy this village for four thousand years?

From this prehistoric past are left two almost indestructible signs. Many hundreds of sarsen stones, most of them now scattered and re-used, and the clear route of ancient tracks still visible even though built over and extended. The oldest recorded maps of Cove in the mid 1700s, show no road came directly into the centre of the village from the north-east. The only road (now Victoria Road) turned away near Elmgrove Road to join Marrowbrook Lane at the bottom of Tower Hill. Within the village three straight tracks converged on the very spot this road avoided, and this same site is where most of these ancient sarsen stones still lie.

Hundreds of these prehistoric stones are concentrated in one garden. Can these stones be all that remains of what was once a temple, or stone circle, built to worship the Sun and chart its yearly passage across the heavens? Whether fact or fiction, and irrespective of what historians or archaeologists may say, it is for the people of Cove to decide if they want to believe in and claim this distant ancestry. Stone circles still exist in Britain made of sarsen stones consistent with the surviving stones in Cove. Huge lintels at different points of the compass are over processional ways.

If you are not quite sure what a sarsen stone looks like, there is no need to go as far as Stonehenge, for a fine example is on display outside Farnborough Parish Church. It was probably taken from the accumulation of stones on Tower hill and placed there over a thousand years ago by the builders of the Saxon church that pre-dated the Norman church built in about 1200. Should you wish to see these ancient stones in their natural surroundings, go to the Chobham Ridge where it all began. For there by the Red Road crossing, a huge sarsen stone was recently unearthed and left by the roadside.

A typical 'lintel stone' now used as a seat outside of Farnborough Parish Church that could have come from Tower Hill, Cove.

Chapter Seventeen
In Conclusion

Perhaps after reading earlier chapters, most people will agree that this small village called Cove has its own strange hidden secrets. Possibly one day a full investigation into its past may be made by some learned Historical and Archaeological Society that will throw more light on points raised in this study made by a strictly amateur historian. All that is included may not be completely accurate or true, so it would be more appropriate had each chapter started with the words "to the best of my knowledge".

Also a time and place must be established, for as I go round the village and talk to other old 'Covites', we often disagree on small details. So to avoid constantly having to add to or alter the script, it has been set out to what is thought to be correct at the moment when pen was first put to paper.

Geological evidence shows that Cove has always stood on a 'spit' of high ground, the approach to which is where the natural surface changes from stony barren ground to rich fertile soil; there is not the slightest doubt as to the nature of subsoil surrounding the 'island' of Cove. This came dramatically to light in the early 1930s when a well-known civil engineering firm undertook the task of installing main drainage and in doing so dug deep enough to break through to the green running sand. This prehistoric hidden water-way flows deep underground beneath and parallel to Cove Brook.

From the very start the trenches dug down the middle of Cove streets were undercut by the wet running sand and began to cave-in, so that in places the hole stretched from front fence to the fence on the opposite side of the road. Other services, like the cast-iron gas and water mains, were left suspended in mid air. Thus the excavations had to be shored up with 12 inch by 2 inch timbers; this shuttering is still in place over sixty years later for the soft sandy clay was so tenacious and clinging that the boarding could not be withdrawn.

For more than a year Cove residents suffered the trauma of roads resembling battle-fields and with pumps running day and night. By Hemmings' corner, where Cove Road joins Bridge Road near West Heath Bridge, there was a hole deep and wide enough to hide a double-decker bus. What was a great inconvenience to many proved an adventure to the children of the village. Nights were lit up by lines of flickering paraffin lanterns and the glowing coke braziers in front of the night-watchman's sentry-box hut. Not all watchmen were grumpy old men, one, a Mr Rutherford who lived at No 19 Tower Hill, was elderly, talkative and well-read, allowing use of his fire for toasting, potato baking and chestnut roasting.

The law required that the night-watchman must always keep alert and awake, not easy when sitting in front of a cosy fire the fumes of which could be over-powering. At one time a man fell asleep across the hot embers and before a passer-by, smelling burning, pulled him off still unconscious the heat had penetrated his clothing scorching his chest and stomach.

The lessons learnt in the 1930s were forgotten when in 1994 another company came along and dug up the same streets and even with the most modern equipment still found trouble. Cove Road was like a scene from a science-fiction film, with an 18 inch thick bright blue plastic 'snake' being fed into a hole and disappearing forever into Cove's primaeval slime. These modern road-works lack the colour and interest of days gone by for there are no longer the night-watchman's cheery fire or the homely oil lamps to compensate for all the inconvenience.

What will archaeologists of the future find beneath Cove village if they dig in a few thousand years time? The seemingly indestructible sarsen stones may still be there, but it is doubtful if any signs of our present homes will survive. For even in a short 50 years, the village has lost and forgotten many fine old houses. Today we can try to imagine the origin of objects that have been found beneath our village: an ancient flint arrowhead, a bronze figurine of an animal or the rusty remnant of an ancient flint-lock musket.

Think then of what a searcher of the future will make of a large mass of metal that may still lay buried on the far side of the airfield. For it was there 60 years ago that a Hawker Fury single-seater biplane-fighter, the predecessor of the more famous war-time Hurricane, failed to pull out of a steep dive and plunged at high speed into the soft grassy airfield, disappearing into a hole only a few feet across. A team of RAF men with shovels dug for evidence, but I think they were more concerned with levelling the surface than digging out the aircraft. Down below there may still be a battered but complete Rolls Royce engine, a fine prize for future archaeologists. The airfield is so altered that although I stood and watched the men dig I have no idea where it might be. But no doubt a good metal detector would pick up a ton of steel buried 6 feet below ground.

A whole bog full of First World War aeroplane relics lie beneath the buildings around the Arrow Road Council Depot, they were thrown away by Royal Flying Corps mechanics working at the then Southern Aircraft Repair Depot along the northern edge of the aerodrome. These are possible historical artefacts of the future. Should any amateur archaeologist want to make a further search for buried objects, I am only too pleased to give approximate locations of those mentioned.

The flint arrow-head, authenticated by a County Archaeologist from Winchester, was picked up on the allotments that were once opposite Weir Avenue. Sceptics may claim this is no proof that it had lain there for thousands of years, when it could have been dropped by a careless collector much more recently. The bronze figure of an animal was dug up from under an old oak tree that stood by the pond in the middle of a small triangular field bordered by Fleet Road, Trunk Lane and the drive up to Trunk House, now Ladywood Avenue, and of course completely built over. Had this figure been moulded in solid gold it would have been universally acclaimed as an important archaeological discovery, but alas it is only forged in humble bronze, the first and oldest metal worked by prehistoric man. Its shape resembles some sort of deer or antelope and as such bears a remarkable similarity to those animals depicted by early man on the walls of deep dark caves in many parts of Europe.

The true 'buried treasure' of Cove is the sarsen stones, worthless, heavy and inexplicable, they are the enigmatic vestiges of a forgotten prehistoric past. For nobody will ever know who placed them here, or why, but they appear to be evidence of a carefully sited centre of observation and ritual connected with the movement of the sun. The whole history of

Bronze figure dug up from beneath oak tree by Trunk Lane.

97

Tower Hill, Cove, evolves around one simple but indisputable fact. That a few hundred years ago men building a small farm cottage could go to a nearby heap of large stones and select some of the right size and shape to form the foundations. Now many years later these same stones are again exposed to the light of day and when placed alongside others are indistinguishable from those that have always lain on Tower Hill. Now outdoors and exposed to all weathers, they are fast losing their top coating of soft white mortar that joined stonework to brickwork forming the outer walls of this old thatched farm cottage.

By just thinking and looking, but taking nothing for granted, one can see signs of the Cove of years gone by. So simple a thing as the length of gardens of houses in Cove Road opposite the 'Green'. This shows that when the 'New Road', now Cove Road, was laid out these plots of building land varied in length for they all ran back as far as the old 'lost' road through the centre of the village. Those houses nearest to Marrowbrook Lane having the longest gardens and at the other end by Yeomans' Pottery opposite Prospect Road each garden gets shorter.

This then concludes the second account of Cove village life to be written over a span of almost a century. The past seventy five years have seen vast changes, from an entirely agricultural community living in many different types of dwellings, both large and small, to the present day spread of red brick, all very similar houses, with never more than four bedrooms. The only large dwellings to be built now are one hundred roomed mansions for the elderly.

Gone are the meadows, streams and ponds; gone too are the old craftsmen, thatchers, wheelwrights and farm labourers. So what will our village be like in another seventy five years? Will there be any scrap of nature's greenery left? Or will Cove Common all turn, like the Southwood fields, into rows of new houses and huge monolithic pseudo-Grecian monuments to modern commerce?

Index